Praise for

This Time Next Year

I have re-read sections of this manuscript (book) twice before putting pen to paper.

The tears in my eyes are drying up as I am writing this. I was on this emotional roller coaster when I was only thirty-seven and would have loved this book all those years ago as I battled back then on my own with very little support.

And I'm now sixty-nine and haven't lived with anyone since! What a wonderful resource manual for women going through any form of heartache and grief from broken relationships.

This book gives you the insights on how to build yourself up with courage and resilience and how to rise bigger and stronger than the person you were before.

Thank you, Jaynie, for the privilege of reading your book.

Heather MacKenzie

Geelong Victoria

Praise for

This Time Next Year

Started reading and it's definitely a great read for me – it gets me in from the beginning … it's light yet has honest depth, it is filled with spark, and I'm genuinely invested in hearing your journey and how it may be relevant to me or someone I know … and that's it's biggest pull! It's soooo relevant to what's happening to so very many people who are lost in old learned conservative ways which no longer serve or appreciate them!!

Joey Moore

TV Presenter & #1 VoiceOver Artiste, AlwaysMore Voice Production

Praise for

This Time Next Year

This is a wonderful book! It reads like a warm conversation with a good friend. Jaynie takes us on a journey of love and healing, sharing insights and tips for us along the way.

Pamela Barnum

International Author
Trust and Body Language Expert
Former Federal Prosecuting Attorney, Canada

This Time Next Year

Also by Jaynie Morris

Against Their Odds

Eternal optimism saved my life!

Redirect & Receive

Your self-love journal

This Time Next Year

YOUR GUIDEBOOK TO LIFE FREEDOM!

Jaynie D Morris

First published in 2023 by JayPal Global Publishing an imprint of Abundantia
Global Group.
PO Box 5274 Middle Park, Victoria Australia 3206
Telephone +61 449 886 788

Text copyright © Jaynie D Morris
Design copyright © JayPal Global Publishing

ISBN 978-0-646-87025-0 (paperback)

With publishing assistance from thestorykeeper.com.au
Typeset by dbtype.com.au

Contents

DEDICATION

I dedicate this book to Muriel Edith Pryde.

Born March 30th, 1925.

Beautiful, intelligent, funny, fearless, independent, fiercely protective and unconditionally loving until the end

February 18th, 2009.

An incredible torch bearer for women over 50 ...

she just didn't realise it.

Thank you Mum, I miss you xxxx

EPIGRAPH

'Why are you wrapping me?' said the caterpillar to its mother.

'I'm not wrapping you ... I am helping you on your journey.'

'But I'm happy here ... creeping around the leaves, doing the same thing every day,' said the caterpillar.

'That's why it's time. Doing the same thing every day, eating the same leaves every day ... that's not what you came to this magnificent world to do,' replied the caterpillar's mother.

'I'm scared,' said the Caterpillar ... 'It's getting dark, and I am sleepy and ... I ... am ... '

All wrapped up and safe away, the caterpillar's mother left.

As the days went by, changes began. Internal and external changes ... some were drastic and others ... well, they were necessary.

Then one day, the little creature began to wake. He was uncomfortable so he wriggled and in so doing he realised he had grown ... and changed.

With each movement, the carefully wrapped cocoon began to tear.

Suddenly, without a thought, the wrapping fell and a beautiful creature with gossamer blue wings flew into the sky, the sunlight catching its silvery body.

Higher and higher it went then in a moment, it looked back … realising that being comfortable wasn't actually being safe. Being comfortable was playing small. Surrendering to the guidance of his mother, in the safety of her love, he had indeed emerged into the magnificence of the world,

Now it was his time … the magic of greatness and adventure lay ahead. Now … in that moment … he understood.

FOREWORD

The first time I met Jaynie Morris was on a phone call. It was one of those moments that are so special that life seems to stand still, and everything is suddenly in glorious technicolour!

What was meant to be a quick business call became a call full of synchronicities, stories, laughter, tears, and the recognition that we were definitely going to be friends for life.

That call was eleven years ago and since then we have travelled all over Australia and to many beautiful places in the world together. All the time-sharing rich conversations that 'deep dive' straight to the heart.

As survivors of devastating marriage break-ups (yes that's plural!), financial loss, betrayals and grief, we have supported each other as we both navigated re-building and re-inventing ourselves.

As Jaynie's dear friend the great motivational speaker Jim Rohn wisely said, 'For things to change, you have to change.'

As I finished reading the last page of Jaynie's book, I was so happy for you – dear reader – as now you have her as your friend too, holding your hand through the grief, loss and chaos of a break down within the pages of this powerful guidebook.

Oh, how I wish I had a manual like this one during the challenges of my own life.

Woven within ten+ simple chapters are personal anecdotes, great advice, compassion and common sense plus much needed doses of humour and love.

This book has been written in the midst of Jaynie's own marriage breakdown and her honesty will connect you, empower you to move forward, and take steps to find the courage, support and pathways to create positive change.

This is the best book I have ever read for women over fifty that are considering leaving their partners or have left their partners. It is a daunting, overwhelming time when everyone in your life will be giving you conflicting advice.

With this book you can begin to navigate your own path to a breakthrough.

It's also the perfect gift for anyone going through the pain of a relationship breakdown.

My wish for everyone who has been broken is to never forget these words: 'Every time a heart breaks, somewhere, something beautiful is being born. Look forward to your own rebirthing.'

With love,

Suzanne Skillen

Internationally Successful Entrepreneur
Make a Wish Ambassador
Golden Octopus Board Member
www.goldenoctopusfoundation.org.au

INTRODUCTION

How is it that one day we are in our 20s and 30s, living our lives not thinking too much about 'tomorrow' and the next day, BOOM! We are over fifty and pondering 'What just happened?'

We saw our parents get aches and pains and we heard the word menopause mentioned now and again but, for us, it was all 'down the road'. Some of our parents or their friends would fight and a few got divorced or even died. However, we didn't pay too much attention to it all. It just wasn't relevant to us. After all, we had Carrie Bradshaw and the girls on *Sex and the City* giving us all the advice an independent woman needed, right?

Then one day, some of us find ourselves on our knees in the middle of a room with crushing pain in our chest as our hearts break and our tears rinse the carpet. Our lives flash by as memories of happy times, times regretted, and opportunities missed scream through our head. Our hot flashes are determined to add to the conflict and refuse to abate as we lean back on a chair and despair at what we think is time left too late – for anything. The hope and joy of *Eat, Pray, Love* now seems incomprehensible.

Sound familiar? When I read the last three paragraphs to some girlfriends over lunch, they each thought I was either writing about them or someone they knew!

Now, I know that life breakdowns happen all the time to women, men, teenagers and children alike however this book is about me and you. It's about we women over fifty. We have spent years feeling we are courageous by not sharing our emotions, feelings and challenges with others for fear we would be judged 'less than perfect'.

I have written this book with the purpose of providing you with a 'map' to help you navigate through any breakdown you may be experiencing in your life.

Why? I often asked myself why I wanted to put pen to paper and write this book and my answer differed every time. Then, one day I realised the explanation was a combination of every answer. Life is a pathway littered in choices. We do far better in life if we have a guidebook, a manual, a map that can help us understand blockages, barriers and detours along the way. When we are more informed, we make better choices.

For example, I wish I had been given a guidebook on how to be a mother. I was a very young mother, having my first child at the age of nineteen. Back in those days there weren't the books, podcasts, apps and online courses that there are today. It was simply a case of, 'here you go, now take care of the baby.' They don't let surgeons take the life of others into their hands and operate without years of research. We shouldn't treat our lives with any less care.

My wish is that within each chapter you find something that helps you with whatever it is you need right now. That might be a relationship breakdown, a health challenge, career issue or perhaps a 'What do I do with my life now?' moment. In each chapter I will share my personal story. I will share the lessons I have learnt along with stories of other women just like us, always showing how to utilise those lessons in your own life.

My hope is that once you finish this book you will feel more clarity in your life and be more empowered to make the necessary changes in order for you to step out of **Breakdown** into your own **Breakthrough**.

Working together let's recover your hope and ignite your desire to restart your life, your way. Let's find where you want to be 'this time next year' and, step by step, map out how you will hit that target!

Awakening

In 2021, my life, once again, changed forever. I say once again because as I look over the decades of my life so far there have been so many 'milestones' that have changed the direction I was going in, and this was yet another one.

As I sat in my rented one-bedroom unit surrounded by a mixture of borrowed furniture and a few pieces I have out of storage, I asked myself a question that I have been asking over the previous twelve weeks, 'How did I get here ... again?'

You see, three months prior to this moment I was living with my then husband in our large home on the beach. To everyone outside of those four walls, our marriage and relationship of over twelve years was a solid one and we were often referred to as a 'golden couple'. However, inside those four walls, the story was often a lot different. There came a point where I had to admit the two of us would be happier and in a much more honest place if we no longer lived together.

I am not the first woman over fifty to experience a marriage breakdown and I am certainly not going to be the last. However, since that day the same question keeps entering my mind; 'How did I get here ... again?' It had to be explored.

'How did I get here … again?' Perhaps you have asked this of yourself too? It could be that a job you were doing didn't work out or perhaps a financial situation went wrong? A relationship with a friend which, for whatever reason, has changed? And of course, one of the most common times we ask this question is, as women over fifty, when we are looking at our life in general and pondered 'What's it all about?' There are so many times in our lives where this question could, and does, come up.

I wonder if it is because so many of we women over fifty grew up in an era that conditioned us to believe once we were married, had children and created a home, we'd live 'happily ever after'. So, when things don't work out, the breakdown feels worse?

At a speaking engagement I attended recently, an audience member shared they had come to a crossroads in their life and felt terribly lost and alone. I was speaking about how women over fifty often feel 'overlooked' and ignored by society when it comes to business. She highlighted the fact that we have been going through this for generations and yet we still don't seem to have the answers, and certainly don't have the tools to really find a way forward.

I know for me I grew up dreaming of a 'perfect life' in every way. The prince charming, the house with the white picket fence, the children, the friendship circles, the 'happily ever after.' I spent hours dreaming of this because in my own life as a child, that was not my reality. In hindsight, I struggled to 'fit in'.

I was the fourth child in my family with many years between me and the others. I've always thought that my earliest memory as a child was the day my family moved into what was to become our family home in Adelaide and how joyous the ensuing years were. As I dig deeper now, I realise that other memories included being lined up against a wall in the family home with my siblings as my parents were in the other part of the home in a loud argument with each other. I remember wondering what was going on and feeling very upset but being comforted by a sister who said it would be ok soon. Other memories of that time included my two sisters yelling at each other and one occasion my eldest sister throwing scissors that narrowly missed my other sister. The 'lovely' memory of the move in day often covered up those painful days.

When I was four my mother and father divorced which left just her and me to 'grow up' together in a time when divorce wasn't the 'norm.' Life at school was often hard, as I always felt like the other kids had the 'perfect family life' and I was an outsider. Creating a life at home that was always filled with opportunity and discovery was my escape. I grew up planning that I would not be like my mother, as amazing, beautiful and talented as she was. I so desperately wanted to 'fit in', to have the life I thought others did. I didn't 'belong'.

I met a wonderful man when I was very young who was my

first husband and the father of my much-loved children. I would definitely say he was my 'favourite husband' despite our age difference (he was eleven years older) and other small challenges, his sense of humour and his personality in general always made me smile. Unfortunately, mistakes were made in the marriage, and we separated, however we remained good friends for the children, often having him pop in unexpectedly as the door was 'always open'.

The breakdown that ensued initially however, was devastating and my first real taste of deep sadness. It was also the first time that I felt the shame and guilt of not being able to have 'the perfect marriage.' Again, I was in a situation where I didn't feel I 'belonged'. I was very young and whilst that isn't an excuse, over the years I have discovered that for any relationship to work, there is always work to be done. Trust, communication, honesty, support and respect are some of the many aspects that are fundamental to a relationship working.

Over the following decades I experienced a couple of long-term relationship breakdowns and none of them got any easier. The heartache and pain from experiencing betrayal, lies, deception and abuse. The hits to my self-esteem and self-confidence were all a part of the time that followed. Now, I pride myself on being an *Eternal Optimist,* but even so, I hit depths of despair that I couldn't get out of for days. Much of this period was a continuation of feeling that I didn't 'fit in' or 'belong'. Now I was questioning why it was so important to feel like I did 'fit in'. For the first time in my life, I was coming to the realisation that in order to be happy and feel complete, I didn't need to 'fit in' so that others would accept me or for that matter even like me. The dawning of understanding that 'belonging' didn't mean being as others expected me to be, or wanted me to be in order to have me in their lives, was profound. And it was just the beginning of the unfolding of the woman I am today.

Breakthrough

So ... returning to the question ... 'How did I get here ... again?' This breakdown in my life has been the hardest and by far the worst, however it is also actually the best!

Throughout my life as an Author, Life Coach and Motivational Speaker I have helped and worked with countless people around the world. I have often heard it said that we learn from others, yet we never learn from our greatest teacher – ourselves!

During the first twelve weeks, I had been feeling shifts and changes that felt like 'awakenings.' Sometimes, I had dismissed thoughts as they had felt too obvious and then I had stopped myself and said 'Wait a minute, if it is so damn obvious then why are you still crying? Why is your heart still breaking and why are you in constant pain?'

So, I decided to embrace the contrast, and this is what I want to share with you, because if you are reading this far then perhaps it is because you are going through a breakdown? Perhaps you are in a time in your life when you are asking yourself 'What am I doing? Where am I going? What is it all about?'

When we have contrast in our life, we are able to see what we want and what we don't want.

For example, if it's a really hot summer day and we are down at the beach feeling hungry. We don't go up to the café and order a large hot, steamy bowl of potato and leek soup with a dash of chili! (Or maybe you do?) We might want a nice cold, icy drink and a big bowl of delicious creamy ice cream!

Same with relationships. Deep down, if we are truly honest, we know what we want and we know what we don't want. It's contrast.

A training I did with world renowned motivational leader, Lisa Nichols, taught me a fabulous way to breakthrough with contrast. It's her take on what personal growth teachers have shared for years. It came to mind during the first few weeks of my breakdown and I love it!

Visualise … now stay with me here … it really does help, and it works.

Our minds, and in particular our subconscious mind, is openly receptive to whatever we feed it. If we are constantly thinking negative thoughts, if we are constantly listening to media that is filled with doom and gloom and if we are spending more time with people who are always complaining, for example, then our subconscious mind thinks that's how we want it to be! So, guess what? It programs everything we think and do to be negative, complaining and fearful of life in general!

As a Master Neuro Linguistic Practitioner (NLP), I am trained to help others clear these negative emotions and beliefs and I love seeing the transformations occur. Yet, throughout my relationship breakdown I forgot it all for myself! My poor subconscious mind was totally confused and having its own internal battle which resulted in my daily 'highs and lows' of emotion!

So, the awakening I have had is to remember the power of visualising by incorporating contrast.

I bought myself a beautiful pink journal and at the end of every night, before I go to sleep, I write down the things that I have done throughout the day and the emotions I have felt. This has often been a challenge in itself as I've found tears dripping over the pages clouding my vision as the pain of some days has been so hard.

Then at the beginning of each day, before I get out of bed just after I have woken up, I take ten minutes and visualise how I would like the coming day to be. I think about the things that I have already scheduled and visualise them all working out well and me being in a calm and peaceful space. I then take a few extra moments and visualise how I would like my new life to be. The home I want to live in, the work I want to be doing, the time spent with my family. I visualise how I want to feel in my body, the health and wellness I want to have and the abundance on every level that I want each day to be filled with. Then I take three deep and slow breaths … and slowly stretch my body and say out loud, 'Thank you!'

This practice, when done every day, resets our subconscious mind, particularly in times of breakdown.

It sends the true messages you want it to receive and the more we do this the more our subconscious mind manifests it. As we become stronger and more resilient, when negativity does come knocking at our door, we grow to deal with it in a much better way. Our subconscious mind learns to protect our mind, body, heart and soul against the naysayers and increases our self-esteem and self-confidence.

Now I am not saying it is going to happen instantly and I know all too well that it has to be done consistently, however as my dearly loved friend, the late great Jim Rohn, always used to say – 'Repetition is the mother of skill' – and waking up from a breakdown and creating an incredible breakthrough is a skill!

We become skilled through practice, practice, practice … and that is what this Contrast Visualisation method is. My teaching of 'This Time Next Year' process emphasises this and has proven to make it happen!

Lesson

As I write this for you, I want to say that the lesson I have learnt with my relationship breakdown is that during the years leading up to it, I lived through many contrasts. Just like you, I often felt that there were times that weren't quite right, however for whatever reason at those times, I chose to ignore it all, wanting my childhood dream to finally be a reality.

The powerful lesson has been that when faced with contrast that creates questioning, it's important to take the time to explore why the contrast is there.

Is it because the unwritten list of what I did want in life … how I did want my life to be … was trying to get through? I am feeling so empowered by this. I know, moving forward, whenever contrast presents itself, I will take the time to explore why it is there before I decide what to do next. Reaction instead of response to anything that challenges us is dangerous. Taking a breath, assessing the challenge and then responding, whilst often uncomfortable, is the path of clarity and aligned outcomes. Contrast in life is our heart helping us see the way.

Let the voice of your heart
Push through the blocks in your mind

CHAPTER 1

To stay or to go?

I have walked away from my marriage and, as I write this chapter, the word 'courage' comes to mind.

Courage because, as a woman over fifty, especially during a global pandemic, it would have been far better to stay in the marriage for reasons of both financial security and accommodation. However, my emotional pain was fast manifesting into physical pain and the 'Jaynie' I used to know was becoming a distant memory.

For quite some time, in fact a couple of years by this stage, a constant internal question was 'stay or go?' Many women tell me they had the same alternatives circling their minds for a long time before they acted. The answer didn't come easily to any of us. In fact, there is never one simple answer. That, I am sure, is why the pain and heartache is so real.

To the 'outside world,' ours was a perfect marriage. Good looking couple, both with happy and generous personalities. A 'love story' set in a large home by the beach. My business was ticking along, maybe not as fast as I would like, but because it was in the 'public eye' my social media looked convincing.

The reality was very different.

Every day something changed, circumstances altered, communication broke down and my husband's past life began to catch up with him and finally reveal itself to me. The global pandemic uncovered so much more than a virus in our marriage. I had a lifelong belief in the strength of my own intuition but I had to berate myself for not following it diligently in recent years. Mistakes I made from time-to-time were confirmation of this. We had planned for me to take a run at politics and I had spent many months working with others to make that happen. However, knowing what I now knew about my husband, I had to let that aspiration go.

Deep down I knew I could only know happiness again if I left but the prospect of the unknown made me feel incredibly vulnerable. My inner Ego, that relentless internal rationalist dedicated to quietening my gut instincts, awoke and filled my mind with all of the practical reasons why I should stay.

'Where will you go? Why would you leave the comfortable

space you are in? Just put up with it. What will you do when you leave? Who will support you? You can't do it on your own. You are a woman. You are over fifty. You will struggle and end up being a sad statistic. Don't you know single women aged over 55 are eight times more likely to be homeless? Just suck it up. Put up with it. Pretend that life is happy and cry in the loneliness of the night. It'll be worth it!' Those last lines were spoken by my mother-in-law when I once shared a frightening example of my domestic situation with her son. Pretending is what she had done in her marriage and it was her recommendation that I do the same. 'Like father like son' she said as she poured another cup of tea.

The power of the Ego! It is the one thing that stops us from breaking free. From admitting that life isn't the way it should be and that we are strong, capable and deserving of love, happiness and freedom! This is when we have to enlist our heart and feed it every day with a 'vision of the future'.

But, what if you don't know your own heart? What if you are too scared to trust your intuition? The first step is for you to discover how your intuition speaks to you. Philosopher and teacher, Jiddu Krishnamurti, once said 'Intuition is the whisper of the Soul.' Each of us experiences our own intuition differently. For some of us it is a 'gut feeling', one that might manifest in butterflies, stomach ache or queasiness. For others it is a 'voice' that quietly seeks our permission to speak. Some might feel it in the breath, a tightness of the chest or a sense of dizziness. Others experience a unique sense of calm and clarity. The possibilities are endless but they all come with a 'feeling' about how to proceed and, once identified, that intuition can be very powerful.

The next step is self-trust. One of the easiest ways to trust your intuition is to think of all the times you did not trust it and how you felt afterwards. Start small with something like a party invitation where your gut told you not to attend because they 'weren't your kind of people' but you went out of politeness and it was a real waste of time. You can build up from examples like that to some of the more significant times you ignored your best instincts. Generally speaking, when you ignore your intuition, you feel uneasy afterwards. Then use your rationalist Ego to look back and see if you would have been better off following your intuition. Also, consider whether you've often ignored the same advice from your body and whether this is manifesting physically in you. Anxiety and even depression can be a sign that you are not living the way you know you should.

Part of trusting yourself is identifying what you are afraid of. Fear is the thief of life and it is the superpower of Ego. Ego uses fear to intimidate us into ignoring our intuition. Fear of disapproval. Fear of loneliness. Fear of failure. The truth is, when our Ego is not dominant, we actually thrive and survive in such an abundant way that anything less is a travesty! Ego would have us spend our lives weighing up the pros and cons of every decision. Evaluating our choices *is* an important process but it is only *part* of the process. To pick a course of action and to follow it through requires instinct, emotion, heart and soul. Making the choice to act is when the change begins.

In summary, think about how your intuition speaks to you. Then, take 10 minutes in a quiet space and write down five times in your life when you had a 'gut feeling' about something but you didn't follow it? What was the outcome? Are there any similarities between each event? Is there a pattern of events? What would have happened if you had followed your intuition? Finally, commit to listening to your intuition in the future. Explore what would happen if you followed it and how you would respond to others in the situation. Write down the worst thing that could happen if you ignore it. Write down the best thing that could happen if you did follow your intuition.

So, let's get started and create *your* plan for 'this time next year'.

Start by taking out a piece of paper and writing down all the things that are not good in your relationship. All of the things that you know you don't want to continue, especially the things that your intuition is telling you hurt too much.

Your list might look something like this:

* Husband's infidelity – I think it will continue and this hurts me emotionally and risks my health.

* Husband's withdrawal – we don't talk and there

is no intimacy. Maybe I have also withdrawn as I
don't find hm attractive any more

* Lack of validation – I am not recognised as
  contributing anything worthwhile. This hurts as I
  like to please others.

* Conflict – when we talk, we fight. We don't agree
  on much. I want peace and quiet.

Follow this with an honest list of reasons why you are staying.
Your list might look something like this:

* Financial benefits – I work part-time and would
  struggle to live on what I earn

* Concern for husband – he has no friends and his
  depression might spiral

* Emotional investment – It was fun at first. I've
  put 10 years into this relationship and hate to
  quit anything

* Social networks – we have the same friends and
  I don't want to lose them

* Unlovable – who else would have me?

Write down when the last time was that you felt totally
happy, fulfilled and excited for life! Dig deep … really deep …
and make sure you find that moment in your life. If you can't
remember a time, then that is another clue!

Then, on another page, write down all of the things you want in your life. Write as if money were no object and everything flowed beautifully. Where you would live, what you would be doing, how your days would unfold. List all the things you want in life, leaving nothing out. Write it all down regardless of whether your mind tells you it is impossible and you can't have it. Bypass Ego's 'voice' in your head and be brutally honest with yourself. And when you are done ... write some more!

Your list might look like this:

* Live in a two-bedroom apartment near the grandkids with a car space

* Buy a nicer car

* Work 4 days per week

* Exercise every day

* Meet a new companion – it might even be platonic but someone to go out with

* Take a holiday in Spain

* Join a book club

In essence you will have created two lists; What would happen if you stay? What would happen if you go? The latter can be the foundation of where you want to be 'this time next year.' It can be your 'Breakthrough Plan'.

Ok, now let's drill down even further. Look at that second list and break down each element focusing on what you need to do to achieve your aspirations. For example, when you leave the relationship, you may need to move out of the home. It doesn't necessarily need to be permanent it could be temporary. Where would you like it to be and what would you be okay with for the short term? How much money would you need to pay for rent and utilities? This all becomes part of your financial budget which we will discuss in another chapter, however hopefully you can see where this new exciting 'to go!' plan is leading you?

Whilst you are doing this there are bound to be moments when you feel overwhelmed? I know, it's a lot! But step-by-step you can achieve more clarity and decide whether to stay or go. Meantime, let me share this meditation with you as it often helps me in times of uncertainty.

A Meditation to Centre You

Find a quiet, safe and comfortable place to either lie down or sit. Make sure you won't be interrupted, turn off your phone and computer as well.

Close your eyes and place the palms of your hands facing up.

Take a nice, slow deep breath in ... hold it ... hold it ... and breathe gently out.

Take another nice, slow deep breath in ... hold it ... hold it ... and breathe gently out.

As you continue this breathing feel the energy from the base of your feet wrap around your lower legs. Feel the warmth and gentleness that surrounds you.

As you breathe in, feel the energy warmly rise up through your legs to surround your hips and stomach ... and breathe out.

Slowly breathing in, feel the warm energy continue to rise up through your chest, around your shoulders, down your arms to your fingertips ... and breathe out.

As you breathe in, feel the warmth wrap around your neck and up into your jaw and cheeks ... breathe out.

Inhale and feel the energy rise through your eyes, around your ears, into your head and breathe out.

As you take a nice, slow, deep breath in ... feel the warm energy building up at the top of your head and as you exhale feel it rise out from the top of your head and cascade all over your body ... surrounding you with love, safety and trust in the power of your intuition.

Sit with this beautiful warm energy for a while and when you are ready, wiggle your fingers and toes and open your eyes.

I invite you to explore the many Guided Meditations that are available on my website www.jayniemorris.com

I have carefully and lovingly created them specifically for women over fifty to be a part of your 'tool kit' for love, life and freedom!

I can see the past
It's not how I imagined it would be
I can't see the future just yet
However, I know that it is there …
filled with possibility

CHAPTER 2

What next?

'What next?' is a daunting concept. So, where better to begin when contemplating your next move than with YOU? Let us work on uncovering what motivates your thoughts and behaviour, the drivers of which often stem from childhood or significant events in your life. Then, let us look at who you really believe yourself to be. Being honest with yourself is the only way to start the next chapter of your life.

I remember my childhood fondly but it wasn't all smooth sailing. My parents divorced when I was 4 and, because this was not the norm, other children were not always kind to me about having a single mum. I had much older siblings but they had long since left home. It was just me and Mum. We basically 'grew up together' and I loved her very much. Unfortunately, there was a dark cloud lurking in the back of my mind as I grew up. It was the nagging feeling that I had been a 'mistake.' I knew my parents had been planning to split when they discovered I was on the way. They initially stayed together but Dad left 4 years after I came along and I only saw him for an hour on Sundays. Deep down, I felt abandoned by my father.

However, in the final days of my father's life we had occasion to spend half an hour alone together and when I raised my suspicion that I was a mistake, his reply was the complete opposite. He said he was overjoyed to discover I was on the way and yes, whilst Mum and he were having their share of issues, that all seemed to fade as a result. He said he couldn't wait to give the news of my arrival to his sister-in-law Jane, and my Aunt Jane confirmed this many years later. She said Dad called her to ask if they could name me after her, and Dad shed tears of joy during the conversation.

Those two conversations were a revelation and critical to my feelings of self-worth, but neither could completely erase the many years I struggled with feelings of abandonment by men. In fact, as I write this, I have just left another counselling session where, as a woman over fifty, I still seek support and insight. These days my counselling is less for the emotional support because I have done considerable work and am in a much stronger place than years gone by. I now go to ensure that if in the future I happen to meet someone, I do not bring that *baggage* along for the ride. I treat the counselling like 'mental health insurance'...it's best to have 'coverage' just in case!

Interestingly, in discussion with other women my age I've learnt that feelings of childhood abandonment are not uncommon. In our early years, separation and divorce wasn't commonplace. Looking back, we all saw the signs of marital distress amongst our parents and, as the 1960s unfolded, more of them chose not to stay in the marriage 'for the sake of the kids'. Many children, like me, were caught in a time where separation did happen but it was not the 'norm'. So, it's no wonder abandonment issues started on a subconscious level and manifested into our lives as we grew.

My mother was a beautiful, amazing, intelligent and charismatic woman. I loved and admired her immensely and people who knew her would often say that I remind them of her. I was proud to say, 'I am my mother's daughter.' However, is that something to be proud of? Whether they like it or not, children are influenced by and often carry the 'traits' of their parents throughout their lives. I love that I have Mum's independence, compassion, leadership qualities, confidence, eternal optimism and innate intuition (or the Fae as they say). I definitely inherited her legs which were great! However, as I got older, I discovered a few other traits of my mother that I wasn't quite as thrilled with, particularly when I would catch myself mid-sentence using her words and tone of voice.

It's these complex layers that make up the tapestry of our lives. However, there comes a point where I often ask myself, 'Who am I, really?' and 'What have I done with my life?' If left unexplored, these questions can lead to deeper issues. So why not give ourselves permission to explore these issues?

From my earliest days in the Personal Development and Life Coaching industry, I noticed an obvious yet 'unspoken' resistance by many to take part. Whilst I had benefited greatly as a 'client' and 'student' of the life coaching industry, it was clear the resistance was due to more than the investment in a session. I often wondered whether it was a subconscious fear that something might be uncovered in a session that would be too hard to bear. Or, was it a fear that the blocks in their lives may well get fixed and they wouldn't know what to do next? It's amazing how many people live with what we call 'Secondary Gain', where people feel safer having a problem than actually fixing it!

Being brave and facing up to who you really are does not mean you have to focus on all the negatives. Quite the opposite. What we 'do next' is dig deep and reclaim our inner resourcefulness, remembering we are confident and capable of 'taking the next step.'

Think about times when you were a child and faced with a puzzle you needed to solve. Or perhaps it was the very first time that you rode a bike. Remember that feeling of getting onto the seat and holding onto the handle bars, excited in anticipation of being able to do what others did. Perhaps you had someone with you holding the back of the seat guiding you. As you pushed the pedals with your feet, the wobbling of the steering wheel would have made you nervous and perhaps you fell over a few times. However eventually, and excitedly, you reached that moment when you were pedalling and steering all on your own and it felt easy! You never forget how to ride a bike once you have done it!

For me, I look back to my high school days. I was only 15 when I decided school had taught me all it could and it was time to leave. I convinced my mother that I was ready to take on the world! Upon reflection, it was the start of a lifelong quest for the answer to 'Who am I, really?' and 'Where do I belong?' It has been during recent times that I have reflected on moments like these in my life where I have naturally been resourceful and most definitely resilient. I share these with you in the hope that you too can take time to reflect on such moments in your life.

In summary, before you contemplate 'What next?' take the time to reflect and write down your responses to the following questions. Your responses do not have to be definitive and they are bound to change over time. It just matters that you think about them.

* What events in life have shaped how I think or behave?

* Have they shaped me in a healthy way or ways I would like to change over time?

* Am I prepared to seek counselling or address them in other, more private, ways?

* When have I felt empowered?

* When have I been resilient?

* Deep down, who do I think I am, really?

As you grow in self-awareness, the path to action becomes clearer and you can begin to plan 'What next?' Once I had decided to turn my back on a relationship of lies and abuse and pursue a life of happiness, a very dear friend, Traci, suggested I ask myself the following questions. They apply to any type of breakdown in life. Especially those moments where you ask yourself 'What am I going to do in my life?'

Who can help?

Assessing who to turn to is probably THE most important step in getting started.

First, I recognized that other women over fifty have gone through what I was about to and that they were still alive! My heartache was enormous but I would survive too.

Next, I made the decision to confide in my closest girlfriend and tell her what was actually happening in my life. I chose her as I knew she would be my confidante plus I was very much aware that she too had been through this. She had not only survived but was living her dream life ... with a new amazing partner! Yes! Despite what others may say, we women over fifty have much to look forward to. Once I had shared everything, she then helped me see the steps forward. She was, and still is, my greatest supporter and what motivational expert, Melanie Robbins, likes to call the '4am Friend!'

Where do I go?

This step differs depending on your circumstances. If your family is usually 100% supportive then I encourage you to take them into your confidence. Staying with family or close friends when you initially leave your relationship may well be the best and safest thing to do.

For me, I didn't want my family knowing and in fact I wanted to limit who actually knew what I was going through as I was concerned how they would react. This made this step far harder for me. By chance, on a particularly horrid day I ran into another girlfriend on the street. I was vulnerable and burst into tears. I opened up to her and she said she knew of somewhere that was available! I cried such happy tears because the universe had delivered ... not only was this affordable it was on the beach, such a healing place for my soul.

What are my rights?

If you are leaving a marriage or a de facto relationship, this next step is critical. Before you go anywhere I strongly advise that you find yourself a good lawyer. They are the 'unemotional umpires' vital for an optimal financial and property settlement and for support and direction when children are involved.If you don't know any, review the Law Council of Australia's website for practitioners in your state or territory.

Again, I was super blessed in this step. My girlfriend confidante had a great referral and once I had spoken with him I felt so much more at ease. I felt some clarity from the emotional 'fog' and pain I was enduring. He explained the initial steps forward and what I needed to get organized. He gave great advice on things that, if I hadn't spoken to him before leaving, I would have regretted after I left. He pointed out all of the things I needed to do before I walked out the door and gave me a boost of strength that I needed in this most vulnerable of times. My needs and expectations were simple and fair and he helped me to take the emotion out of future dealings. I am not a vindictive or mean person and all I wanted in this step was a fair and swift end.

Unfortunately, as time ensued it became clear that the Family Court is challenging at best and destructive at worst. Women are not supported in the current system and it is vital that your choice of legal representation is the best you can afford.

Lawyers however aren't cheap so if money is an issue, I strongly recommend that you contact your local community legal centre, The Women's Legal Centre in your state or your local Legal Aid agency. In Australia you can also call the Family Relationship Advice Line on 1800 050 321 for free advice on separation and referrals to local services.

If the thought of talking to a lawyer intimidates you, I urge you to look at the websites of divorce lawyers. They usually itemise the initial steps you can take on your own and they outline what the process of seeing a lawyer involves. You can also visit the Commonwealth government websites of Services Australia and moneysmart.gov.au where you will find lots of practical resources. Just reading about it may allay some of your fears.

What will I take?

This advice was vital in the lead up to my final moments in my relationship. All too often I have heard women say they forgot to take important family possessions when they left such as photo albums and parents' mementos. Hopefully, your partner won't be vindictive about what you take ... life is too short to be silly about objects. However, from my research with clients and friends some partners feel the need to 'hurt at all costs' and, unfortunately, that was also my experience.

Making a list of all of the things that you would hate to leave behind is so important. The day before you leave, check everything off the list so you feel confident in the future. Now, I will say that it is incredibly important not to have things on that list that belong to your partner. No matter how bad the relationship was or is, there is no reason to be vindictive or cruel. Taking things out of spite is only taking the pain and toxicity with you! That is not your objective. Your objective is to start afresh and regain your freedom and your life. When I left, I only took what was mine and in fact my partner was left with 80% of the household goods and chattels! I didn't even have a fridge (and at the time we had 3 plus a bar fridge!).

Remember not to leave anything off the list. I made that mistake and left much loved and treasured Christmas decorations and cards kept for generations in my family. They and some of my grandfather's furniture built with his own hands became a 'casualty' at the local dump due to my ex-partner's vindictiveness. If you and your partner are struggling to divide the assets you can contact a Family Dispute Resolution Centre near you. Some are government funded and others are private.

Whilst the advice above may appear to be quite clinical, it needs to be. At this point in our lives, when we are in the 'thick' of it all, our emotions are high and, let's face it, there is no chance of thinking clearly. My experience has also shown that you need to 'revisit' this list regularly and at the final mediation stage ensure that the 'list' is well and truly included. I made that mistake and it contributed to an even greater financial and property loss for me than expected.

Considering these 4 questions are not the only steps to take, however, they are a great place to start. They will help you take the steering wheel and push those pedals to confidently move forward … like everyone else! It's another step forward in your 'This Time Next Year' process.

POINTS TO REMEMBER

* When you are surrounded by personal 'chaos', the overwhelm is real. Taking the moments to close your eyes and breathe deeply is so important.

* Giving yourself 'permission' to move forward is the 'gift' you give your future self.

* Making 'lists' is critical.

* Put 'to be completed by … ' next to each item on the lists.

* Ask for help! People want to support you.

ACTION STEPS

* Think about the reason you started reading this book.

* Underline the information you feel makes sense for you to act on

* Write down what your life would look like if you took these action steps.

* Read what you have written above every morning before you get up and every night before you go to sleep.

When I worry less about 'what if'
And focus more on 'what can'
My financial freedom will align
With ability and opportunity!

CHAPTER 3

Why wealth matters

It's the 'elephant in the room'; Money! The truth is that we all want to be financially debt free, financially independent and financially abundant. Be honest. If you knew that no one was going to judge you, try to take you down with negativity or worse yet – be jealous of you for saying what they feel – you would say out loud 'I want to be 100% financially abundant and debt free!'.

Take a moment now. If you can, go to a quiet place where no one will hear you and then at the top of your voice and 'fist pumping' into the air shout out 'I am 100% financially debt free, financially abundant and financially independent!!!!!' Feels good, yes?

So, why is it that most of us lie to ourselves about this? Perhaps you worry that if you achieve wealth abundance that you will lose friends? Or perhaps you have family members who have negatively put you down and been unsupportive when you have declared you are going to start a new side opportunity to create extra income? Or, perhaps you yourself feel that people with financial abundance are greedy, smart-arse, 'takers'?

Growing up in a single parent home and looking back now, I never heard my mother put down those who had more than we did. I saw her constantly finding ways to be able to pay for things that we needed outside of the basic living costs, showing me at all times that there was 'always a way' and 'always an opportunity to achieve what we want in life'. She instilled in me a belief in myself and she taught me to filter negativity because it never served a purpose for growth in life. My mother wasn't an overly religious person, although going to church regularly and playing the church organ for services was a passion of hers. She loved to sing. She had the most sensational voice and together we would often sing at home around the piano. She taught me how to harmonize and gave me the gift of loving music. Every now and then, and often with impeccable timing, she would quote something from the Bible that was the perfect answer to a question I might have. One of her favourites when it came to finding a way to earn money to buy something special was – 'Seek and Ye Shall Find'.

Believing in myself and my ability to manifest in life is something I have always valued. It's part of each and every one of us, however, for some reason, not all of us embrace it. I've certainly had my times in life where I have 'forgotten' and it has always taken me to a dark place. Depression is my indicator that I have temporarily stopped believing in myself.

I remember speaking at a convention in the USA to an audience who sought the means to create a better life for themselves and their families. I had been asked to talk on how to create a vision for the future and actually manifest it into reality. It's a topic that I LOVE to teach and I know that many LOVE to hear it. However, it's funny how even though in the moment I see 'lightbulbs' going off in the audience, I know that very few will actually walk out of the convention centre and put into practice the simple steps I have taught. Why? Research shows we know what we want and we know what we don't, however, our conditioning in life, such as our family background, our current environment, society, country or governments, often create subconscious blocks that prevent us from moving forward. It's those 'blocks' that I am passionate about removing for everyone. In my NLP Practice I always start with clients on clearing Negative Blocks and Beliefs before we do any other work. Guess what? More often than not, once we have done that (which usually happens in only 2 sessions!) the challenges they have come to see me about are gone and … work done!

Financial security is so incredibly important to us especially in the 'age' we live now. Without it, fear, anxiety, depression and many of life's' challenges fill our heart, mind and soul. As a woman, I experienced the value of money early in my first marriage. About 3 months after we married, I discovered I was pregnant with our first child. Whilst this wasn't planned, we were both excited especially as my husband was 11 years older than me and he was definitely ready to start a family. About a week after we found out, I started getting pains and was rushed to the hospital where I had trained to be a nurse. It wasn't long before the doctors let us know I had a 'threatened miscarriage'. The scare of this was overwhelming and the doctors had me stay in hospital for a week and then said I couldn't work for the remainder of the pregnancy to ensure that everything continued well.

This immediately put us into a financial challenge. My Husband and I were both working at the time and saving to buy a house. His work in the music industry didn't pay a lot however mine in radiology paid quite well. Now it was gone. After a long discussion, we decided that he would look for a more secure, higher paying job, hopefully still in the industry he loved and knew.

This was my first taste of financial struggle. However, this was also the beginning of me learning how to 'make do' and get creative. I remember my mother reminding me that whilst I thought we were in 'struggle city' and not going to be able to buy a home as we had planned, that it was a great opportunity for me to explore what I could do whilst I was pregnant and after the baby was born that would add to our wealth creation and enable our first home dreams to become reality. This was my first exposure to direct sales and the concept of residual income. It is an industry that I have researched a lot over my life and had the good fortune to be in senior corporate roles of major international direct sales companies. It is an industry I am passionate about teaching others the benefits of, especially when creating residual income strategies. I strongly recommend exploring it as part of your 'This Time Next Year' process and have included it in my 'This Time Next Year' Online Course.

When we are at the point of breakdown in relationship, career or life circumstances in general, money is the #1 fear that stops us from leaving and creating a life of happiness. Especially we women over fifty as we hear all of the stories of 'lack', 'struggle', and other negative words. Often times in challenging relationships, we are also subjected to 'control language' from our partners regarding money which adds to our mental thoughts of insecurity. It's known as coercive control and is an increasing factor particularly in domestic abuse. This contributes to our vulnerable state and eats away at our self-esteem and self-confidence.

It's at these times that again we need to dig deep and remember that we are resourceful and resilient! In speaking with other women, I have heard fantastic tips that I want to share with you here.

Be inspired by others!

There is not a day that goes by that there isn't a post on social media or a story on the television that inspires! My 'go to' for inspiration is always books and podcasts. When it comes to our fears of financial insecurity and struggle, I strongly recommend that you do some investigation and Google 'inspiring women over 50'. You will discover hundreds of stories of women just like us who have had terrible things happen in their lives and have lost everything, only to find a way to turn it all around and be financially secure and living their dream lives!

Internationally best-selling author Lisa Nichols is one of those people. She was in huge financial debt and had a young son. Her story of how she took a few things that she knew she could do well and turned everything around is so inspirational! There are so many things you could start doing now, even part time, that could begin to help you financially.

When you are in the breakdown phase everything seems impossible. I know that because even as resourceful and confident as I have been throughout my life, there have been times when my self-esteem and self-confidence have been so eroded by others, that I doubted whether I'd ever to be happy and stress free again! That is when we need to enlist others! Inspiration-from-afar! It's all part of your 'This Time Next Year' process!

You've paid taxes — now use them!

As a woman over fifty there have been many times when we have worked and paid taxes. When we are vulnerable and need to make a huge life change, it is time to explore how those taxes can help us.

If you think you might need support, contact Services Australia (or your local government service) for a confidential conversation about whether you are entitled to government payment or services.

I have known women who were too proud to do this, only to discover when they became super desperate that there was so much available to them. They wished they had enquired sooner! You may be eligible for housing support, financial support (even if only temporary … it all helps), healthcare support and so on. Put it on your 'to do list' and make the call. There is NOTHING to be ashamed of or feel guilty about. You would be surprised at just how many 'well known' people have been down this path too and taken advantage of this, as they should. In not taking this step, you are denying your own self-worth and potentially putting yourself in an even darker place. Don't delay with this part of the process … you deserve it.

However, if you are already receiving government support, be sure to advise Services Australia of any changes to your circumstances such as relationship status, income and change of address. In fact, everyone should keep their MyGov accounts up to date with any changes in status, even an address change, so we don't miss out on important information.

If your finances feel out of control you can seek free financial advice from a financial counsellor. Many not-for-profit organisations can offer advice. A financial counsellor will assess your situation, help negotiate with government agencies, utility providers and other creditors, and refer you to other help. Their services are free. Anyone that poses as a financial counsellor but requests payment is what is known as a debt consolidation and refinancing company. If you do decide to roll all your debts into one consolidated loan with such a company, above all, ensure the company is licenced and, again, seek advice first from a counsellor.

Finally, be aware that you can also ask your lawyer if you are entitled to spousal maintenance. Pursue every avenue for financial support – you deserve the best!

Ask!

When you are putting your list together of what you need, you may find that you need some money up front to get yourself settled. If you don't have it available to you at that point, this is when you need to swallow your pride and ask a trusted friend of family member if they are able to help you.

I was speaking with a woman recently who was worried that her friends may reject her if she asked for financial help. Yet when she did ask, they were more than happy because all they wanted was her happiness. What she did, I recommend you do as well. She and her friends wrote up a 'contract' that clearly stated the amount that was loaned, the date and purpose of the money, and a repayment plan. They had it witnessed by a Justice of the Peace and both held copies. You can do this too and I feel strongly that it is an empowering process. It's incredible how doing things like this add to your strength as well!

It is also important to seek financial management advice. If you have an accountant, I recommend you arrange a confidential meeting with them. Share with them the very real possibility of your relationship breakdown and ask for financial advice on what you should be doing now in order to ensure at least some sort of financial security in the future. Also speak with your bank manager and again confidentially, share the circumstances. These simple steps are often overlooked so it's important to have them on your 'to do list'!

If you do decide to separate or divorce, advice from your lawyer, accountant or banking institution will vary depending on your circumstances. However, generally speaking these are some of the tasks you might want to address:

* Collect all your important documents such as passport, birth certificate, driver's licence, car registration, utility bills. You may need them for identification purposes or to advise them when your circumstances change.

* Itemise what you own together, making special note to what you own outright and what is associated with loans. Note whether the loans are held separately or together.

* Consider your personal and financial security by changing all of your passwords.

* Open a separate bank account in your name.

* Close any joint bank or credit card accounts.

* Cancel any overdraw facilities on your bank account, mortgage or loans.

* Work out how you will pay your mortgage until you have finalised the property settlement.

* If the home is not in your name, discuss with your lawyer whether you need a caveat over the property.

* Remove your name from any joint utility bills which you are no longer responsible for.

* If you are renting, advise your agent or landlord

of your change in cricumstances and ensure the lease contract reflects it accurately.

* Update your will and powers of attorney, particularly after the settlement or divorce is finalised. If you do not have either in place consider establishing them after your separation or divorce is finalised.

POINTS TO REMEMBER

* Financial support and security in the first 6 months after you leave is vital.

* Write a list of all of the things that you have 'joint' responsibility for.

* Include bank accounts, mortgages, rental agreements, utilities, loans, credit cards

* Open up a bank account in your own name.

ACTION STEPS

* Seek out the stories of others who have gone through what you are going through and listen/read/watch

* Contact your government support services and other support organisations and write their details down. Write down all of the questions you have first, on what advice they can give you on what you are entitled to receive

When I make a plan
And it doesn't work out
I'll make another plan
With the changes I have learnt

CHAPTER 4

'Once I was lost ... now I am found'

Have you ever heard the term 'Best laid plans ... '? It comes from a line in a Robert Burns poem 'The best laid plans of mice and men often go awry'. He wrote the poem over 200 years ago about a mouse whose nest was destroyed by a plough she never saw coming! Doesn't that ring as true today as it did back then? How often have you had every intention of getting something done or of things going a certain way, only to be blindsided by the unexpected?

Writing this part of my book is one of those times. You see

this book has been inside my soul for such a long time. It sits in the 'Library within my mind' on the shelves of several unwritten books that eventually will be released into the world! At its core, it is the story of my marriage breakdown which isn't an uncommon thing in todays' society however each breakdown holds within it inspiration for others on what to look for, what not to do, what indeed to do, how to navigate and if at all possible...how not to get to this point in life as a woman over fifty.

So here I am on Day 3 of a long public holiday weekend. I had the plan that on Day 1 of the weekend I would review my notes and let my creative thoughts flow fast and furiously onto the paper...all with the intention of at least 2 chapters done and dusted! When I woke up, I was excited and filled with the anticipation of achievement.

Then, I heard an unfamiliar noise. It was the sound of our family dog whom my son thought could keep me company over the weekend. My GrandFur Baby often comes for sleepovers. She is a beautiful Australian Kelpie with the best nature and personality.

Side Note – if you have a dog when you are in a breakdown stage of your life ... love them more than ever! If you don't have one and are in a position to have one ... get one! Fur babies are THE best mental tonic ever!

She had heard me stirring and had her own plans for the start of the day. So, beach walk it was...and then, I told myself, writing the rest of the day. One thing leads to another (actually 10kms worth) and 2 hours later I was at my computer...finally.

Taking a moment to check social media (because of course THAT was important to my writing...not!) and then surrounding myself with my inspirational pieces on the desk...I began. As I did a short meditation to get my alignment sorted, I opened my eyes and looked at the screen. Then I looked out the window and back at the keyboard. I typed 'CHAPTER'...and then my mind went blank. Sitting there for at least 30 minutes struggling to find the words or thoughts that I knew were inside me but not ready to come out and play, frustration set in.

I felt the overwhelm inside my stomach start to rise up into a well of emotion and the tears flowed like Niagara Falls. 'Why am I even doing this? Why am I bothering? No one wants another 'self-help book' based on breakdowns in life! Who cares about the devastation, lies, betrayal I've endured in relationships? How could I possibly put into words all of the lessons and the breakthroughs that have now allowed me to see that, even as a woman over fifty, life isn't over!' Then came the big one, 'I can't do this! I am useless and can't do anything! There is no more time!'

As I turned off my computer, I resigned myself to the fact today was not the day. I decided to take the pressure off and do what I would advise others in this situation to do. I put everything away that had anything to do with what I had planned. I sat quietly for 10 minutes and breathed deeply, allowing thoughts to flow in and out. Then I did something completely different for the rest of the day and night...not giving the plans another thought.

The next morning was a duplication of the day before, however, this time my GrandFur Baby had even more energy and we extended our beach walk by another kilometre ...which was wonderful.

This time, as I sat down and went through my writing preparation routine, I double checked my notes and realised that I didn't have to do anything 'in order'. I understood that being creative is about allowing inspiration to meet the moment and trust that everything aligns when it is ready. It was the 'action' that was important, not the 'order'.

Gabby Bernstein (world renown spiritual leader and self-help author) refers to this as 'inspired action' and she is right! That is what I did and, as the words flowed across the pages, the joy within my soul had me in such an excited and happy space for the rest of the day! When I went to bed that night I felt great. I had achieved something very special that would help women over fifty in some way. Most of all, my self-belief and self-worth had increased purely by taking small steps towards my large goal.

Your plan won't always be right!

My story here highlights what may well happen when you are putting your plans together for taking 'the next step' out of your relationship. When you are experiencing a 'best laid plans … ' moment and things don't appear to be going to plan, don't lose faith. We are so vulnerable at these times and we can easily fall back into complacency; the 'It may be more comfortable just to stay in this relationship and put up with it' mentality.

It happened to me on many occasions. Furthermore, other people can also behave in a way that makes you feel 'why am I even feeling unhappy anyway?' It's an illusion and your Ego playing tricks on the reality of the situation. This is when you need to be gentle with yourself. If what you had on your 'to do list' gets side-tracked or if you don't get an outcome that you were hoping for, take a break. Put everything aside for the time being and ease the pressure off yourself. Your body will be running on adrenaline anyway so this is the time to nurture yourself and know that what you are doing is trending toward your goal even if it does not feel like it today.

Today may not be the day for it all to fall into place. There may be other factors at play. The universe never reveals itself exactly the way we think it should. So, be kind to yourself and most importantly … breathe.

If in doubt ... don't!

It's important to identify 'doubt' as opposed to 'resistance'.

Meditation is such a great tool to utilize in these moments. I never used to be able to meditate, in fact I thought I was crap at it! The problem was ... I hadn't actually ever tried! I use to think it was sitting cross legged chanting for hours.

What I have learnt since studying and becoming a Master NLP Practitioner and TimeLine Therapist© is that guided meditation works for me! I love exploring Guided Meditations online and there are hundreds of thousands to choose from. I have learnt the art of taking others through Guided Meditations now as well and offer these through my personal business as well as my online courses. If you are feeling doubtful or lacking self-confidence, then I recommend starting to listen to guided meditations on self-confidence daily. I particularly love Glenn Harrold, Marianne Williamson and Dr Joe Dispenza and credit them all for the strength I have gained through their work.

I have created and developed a series of guided meditations that I found were perfect for me and as others have used them, they have told me how these meditations have helped them. I continue to create and share so I invite you to check them out at my website www.jayniemorris.com. I offer them to you as my gift and recommend you visit the site regularly for new ones that may, in the moment you seek, be of value to you.

POINTS TO REMEMBER

* Don't 'beat up' on yourself if at the end of any day you feel you haven't made progress

* Plans change and sometimes that is for the better

* Be openly receptive to all creative solutions

* Trust you intuition! If in doubt...don't!

ACTION STEPS

* If you have done meditation before, then write down the top 3 meditations you enjoy

* In your diary (I strongly recommend you create one, it will help bring 'order to chaos' when overwhelm happens) make a daily 'appointment' with yourself to spend some time and enjoy one of the meditations

* Write down 3 things in your life that you remember laughing and having fun doing

It's only human to want to fill a void
Our soul wants us to make sure
We fill it with self-love!

CHAPTER 5

Stuff it!

Navigating my way through this separation, I told myself I have been through this before and I can make it. At other times, I had to admit to myself, it was a very long time ago and, to be honest, I didn't recall it being as heart-numbing as it was this time around. Perhaps it's because this relationship was longer and I genuinely thought it was the 'forever' one. That's not to say that I didn't think my other relationships weren't, on the contrary. Each time I have been in a long-term relationship I have invested my heart, soul, mind and body into both it and the future possibility. I feel that this time because of the circumstances surrounding the breakdown, I often 'ignored' my feelings, hoping things would change and telling myself I could 'manage' it.

Every night I would go to sleep promising myself that I won't think about it first thing when I wake. However, it was a battle. Some of my research has uncovered that this too is a common problem. The grief of a love lost and the unveiling of the reality is often overwhelming. On good days, my strength and courage that lie wrapped within my eternal optimism and excitement for life in general got me through. On my bad days, the tears and wailing were uncontrollable and the pain within my body deep. We all do it, we all feel it and sometimes the struggle feels never ending.

A client recently said that she didn't understand how some women lost a lot of weight when going through a breakdown! She said all she does is live in her refrigerator! I was the same, often finding myself reaching for food as the 'solution'. On a subconscious level we feel that food will fill the 'void' of emptiness and loneliness inside. It's as if our thoughts of 'more food' will make the pain go away.

Confession – and alert – the following has been a fact for me! I usually started with an extra-large serving of a healthy dinner (at least I start right) and then away I would go! Handfuls of dark chocolate liquorice bullets (convincing myself with every mouthful that the dark chocolate is healthy!) Followed by fruit salad topped with full cream ice cream instead of my usual chia almond milk pudding! More chocolate...more ice cream and then it hits me! The message to my brain that my stomach is finally so full I am going to be sick! Remorse and shame at what I have done envelope me. I promise myself I won't do it again and even try to fool myself that when depression and grief next enter my mind that I will meditate it away!

I know it wasn't my fault but I do take responsibility for my role in the relationship breakdown. If I'm totally honest, I also forgive him on some level, for if I don't then the 'poison' created by what he did will flow through my veins for the rest of my life. I take comfort in remembering the good times we did share. In hindsight knowing the truth about the relationship now I am sure it was all a charade but I have to release those sad and heartbreaking memories.

Food has been my saviour at times and stuffing it all down has allowed me a false sense of 'make it go away' enter my mind. Fortunately, I am understanding that food is never the answer and that self-love, self-respect and trust in my own ability to create life is the only way to peace and happiness ... one day at a time.

Treat yourself ... don't make yourself sicker!

If my personal story with food during this time of relationship breakdown sounds familiar, then once again we are kindred spirits! As I wrote this chapter, I remembered other times where I have used food to 'fill the void' of unhappiness and they weren't always just in relationship breakdown. And if I am to be perfectly honest, it wasn't always food! There have been plenty of times when I felt that a glass of wine or a martini would make the pain go away! The key during relationship breakdown is to be aware of this. It is ok to 'fill that heartache' with food however always in moderation.

Our health is so important and, in such a prolonged stressful time, we need to 'fuel' our bodies with healthy food so it can maintain its good health and strength.

Discipline ... come on you can do it!

With everything else that is going on in our life during relationship breakdown, asking ourselves to be disciplined with what we eat and drink can be tough. So, this is what I did, perhaps you might also like to try it. I wrote down a daily commitment plan for health. I promised myself I would find at least 30 minutes every day to go for a walk ... a fast walk. It gets the endorphins going and your mind gets clearer. Research has shown that this is a vital step (pardon the pun) for helping our general mental health, so during a breakup it's critical to make ourselves do some form of daily exercise. It's gold! And the good news is, it can also set up another new lifestyle choice for you to take into your new future – adding to your 'This Time Next Year' process in a productive and beneficial way!

I also committed to drinking at least 2-3 litres of water every day on top of my herbal teas and my indulgent almond chai latte! Fluids are crucial to good health ... the pure fluids not alcohol. The Mayo Clinic recommends 2.7 litres per day for women (20% of which is likely to come from your diet) but just how much is right for you will depend on your environment (if it is humid, you need more), level of exercise (if you're active, you need more) and health (if you have a fever, you need more). A good gauge is your urine. If it is clear or light yellow you are probably getting enough.

As a Naturopath and Health Professional, I understand the importance of good nutrition so I reviewed the foods that were good for stress, detox and cleansing and made sure I incorporated them in my meals every day. Doing these small things ensured that at least my health was being nurtured and, in turn, I was creating a solid 'insurance' for my body. If you don't come from a health background, talk to your GP about which positive first steps you can take for your health. Even if you decide to get some basic checks done such as see your dentist for a check-up, get your bi-annual mammogram and bowel screening test done or maybe get your lipids and cholesterol checked. Just taking these steps can remind you that your health matters and you deserve to put your health first.

POINTS TO REMEMBER

* The grief of a love lost and the unveiling of the reality is often overwhelming – make sure you allow yourself to grieve.

* Your health is the #1 priority in your life.

* Give yourself permission to flow with the overwhelm and not hold it all in – deep breathe as much as possible when you feel the overwhelm coming on

* Deep breathing won't always be the answer so in those times, give yourself permission to eat those treats if it makes you feel better for a while.

ACTION STEPS

* Write down the things you would like to be doing if you were 100% fit and healthy

* Start a 'Food and Drinks Diary'. At the end of every day for 7 days, write down everything that you ate and drank on that day including the time of day.

* At the end of 7 days, review it and highlight the things that you didn't like or that your body 'reacted' too as well as the things that you did like.

* Make a list of all of the healthy food and drink that you enjoy and start to incorporate that in your daily health routine

When we feel alone
It's a temporary loss of purpose
When we ask for help
We allow others to remind us
what it is

CHAPTER 6

You are not alone

Have you ever shared some challenges you are going through with your friends and had them say – 'I am here for you ... you are not alone?' It's something that I always say to my friends when they are feeling safe in my presence to pour out their issues, indecision and general life challenges. I say it because I genuinely mean it. It's in my DNA to always want to help others in any way that I can. I am pretty sure it is because my life wish is that everyone is happy, and my eternal optimism is my driving force.

So then why is it that when we are on our own with our Ego and mind overwhelming our inner emotions of fear, grief and pain do we not pick up the phone and call our friends to take them up on their offer of friendship love?

Recently I had this moment in my life. I had woken up with a not-so-great feeling. I shrugged it off because the other responsibilities of the day had to be addressed. I told myself there was no time to work any negativity out ... I could do that later. As the day progressed and the distractions of work and family subsided, I found myself driving home in my car becoming overwhelmed with grief and loneliness.

My husband and I had been parted for 9 weeks at this point and the separation issues were taking their toll. As I drove towards where I was staying, I felt the heartache and emotions building once again. These 'waves' always come and go but being aware of it doesn't make it any easier in the moment.

Not long after arriving there, I hit rock bottom. I felt it rising and knew I was about to lose it, so I raced around and pulled all the blinds down, closed the doors then fell to the floor in the foetal position and sobbed hard and deep ... water pouring out of my eyes as if there was a tap behind them.

Pain enveloped my entire body and I called out to God. 'Please God, you know I am not a vindictive woman. You know that I always want what is fair and right. You know that all we should be doing is getting it sorted and move on to live good lives. Please God! I need a miracle. I can't take this anymore!' The tears, pain and prayers were an 'out of body experience' that seemed to go on for hours. Eventually the sobs subsided and I sat myself up against the red velvet chaise lounge. I sat there in silence and had no thoughts within me at all. I was completely empty and void of any emotion.

I got up and fell back into the daily routine, aware that I had finally hit a point in my life where I was done, even though I was still unsure what 'done' really meant. I felt the pain and grief of years of betrayal, lies and abuse. I had kept it contained within, hidden, and worst of all, ignored on so many levels.

About 30 minutes later I received a text message from a dear friend. It was a comedy video clip with the words, 'This is funny, enjoy'. She was right, it was funny, and I sent her back the message, 'Timing is everything … just been on the floor sobbing in the foetal position … this has made me laugh thankYOU xx'

Later that evening she called me and we talked for over an hour, mostly about the common 'world topics' she and I love to discuss. Towards the end of the call, she enquired after my earlier 'adventure on the floor'. I explained what had happened and also what was going on (or to be more accurate – what was not going on) with my separation.

She listened patiently and intently and then she offered the most profound advice for regaining my strength and personal power in the situation. She reminded me I was allowing outside circumstances to 'bully and control me' and that now was a great time to fairly and firmly take back control. She pointed out if I wanted it sorted, I would have to get it sorted … myself!

We laughed so much at the simplicity and accuracy of what she was saying. We chuckled at how I, a fully qualified life coach, was missing the most important aspects of my own personal life at this time! Girlfriends! They are the best 'mirrors' ever!

As I hung up the phone I was filled with excitement! I was exhilarated and confident in who I am and what I am capable of. I was no longer the 'victim'. In fact, I was clear and positive about how my husband and I could get things addressed and sorted now! I realized also that by taking responsibility and not languishing in the pain of loss, I was indeed seeing the lessons the relationship breakdown presented to me.

I also remembered that I am not alone, there is always someone somewhere who has a 'key' to the lock that opens the doors of our soul to greatness.

Finally, and most importantly, as I went to bed and started writing in my journal, I heard my mother's voice say, 'Ask and you shall receive'. Indeed, earlier that day I had let go and asked God for a miracle. My girlfriend was sent, and the miracle was received.

Ask, ask and then ask again!

We have discussed this earlier, however, I can't emphasise enough how important getting help from others is. It is so important before, during and after a relationship breakdown. My moment of pleading on the lounge room floor demonstrates the desperation we experience throughout relationship breakdown. Trusting that if we are openly receptive, the answers will come is so important. In this instance, once again, a dear friend unknowingly helped me.

Gabrielle Bernstein has a great saying 'Be openly receptive to creative solutions.' I love this mantra and it is one that I include in my morning mantras as I get out of bed. Not being attached to the outcome and releasing to the universe has a powerful effect. It is also true of our girlfriends. Those amazing goddesses in our lives just know the right things to say when we need them. Trust.

Support in all forms!

Now, whilst my story here illustrated a girlfriend's help, support in our dark times can come in many ways. If you find yourself in a desperate state and you have no one around, go online. Yes, I know it sounds crazy, however, trust me. The internet can be your friend at this time! Type in 'Inspiring

Women Over 50 TEDx Talk'. I discovered so many incredible women over fifty talking about so many different topics and challenges we face, and each one is only 15 minutes long! If you haven't already tried this, do it now. I really want to know how you go. If you discover a woman who inspires and helps you in your particular situation, please let me know! They can become your 'virtual' girlfriends and will always be there when you need!

Social connectivity is vital!

Research shows that social connectivity is a vital component of living a good, healthy and long life. Since 1938, the Harvard Study of Adult Development has been collecting data on what makes people's lives flourish. It's the world's largest long-term study to determine what creates happiness and, for over 80 years, it has shown that the most important ingredient in health is not career achievement, material success, physical exercise or diet. The most consistent finding is that positive relationships with family, friends and community keep us happier and healthier and help us live longer. So, don't let the breakdown of one relationship (even if it is your most central one to date) jeopardise your health. Get out there and nurture the other important relationships in your life. When we are going through hard times, in particular relationship breakdowns, being 'social' is often the last thing we want.

However, at this time connecting with others, being involved with social events no matter how small or short, can be the difference between prolonged anguish and heartache, and taking a step forward to freedom and a better life.

POINTS TO REMEMBER

* Emotions and internal pain from breakups can often 'cloud' your ability to start taking steps forward

* Whilst you may think that you are alone and have nowhere to turn, it's important to know that you are not alone.

* Now more than ever, you need a support network.

ACTION STEPS

* Write a list of all the people that you know personally.

* Highlight the names of those on the list with whom you are normally most in contact.

* Put a star next to the names of the 'highlighted' people who you feel most comfortable talking to and then every day, call or reach out to just ONE of those people and simply talk. You will be surprised how this benefits your mental health PLUS you may get some ideas and/or extra support in your steps moving forward.

My greatest ideas and gifts
Come to me in the
Silence of the night

CHAPTER 7

The middle of the night

Throughout the 'breakdown years', that is the years leading up to my separation, the 'drip by drip' from the tap of intuition kept attempting to get my attention but my Ego would fight to retain control and maintain the illusion of 'happy ever after'. It meant insomnia became a constant in my life. Many of my clients have experienced this too and whilst it was often attributed to other 'life challenges', in hindsight it uncovered a much-ignored intuition.

Initially I drew upon my naturopathic training and utilized herbal teas, supplements and 'early to bed reading' routines. These were successful to a degree, however, with any increasing negativity, the positive effects were withdrawing and sleep continued to elude me.

Not one for pharmaceutical support, I found myself in a pool of tears at my trusted doctor's office one day. He sat patiently and waited for the pain and tears to subside and then he said to me, 'Jaynie I know that you are not keen on medication however I am concerned how this increasing lack of sleep and stress may impact on your overall health. I don't want any issues with your liver again, and we both know how stress can cause that. Would you consider sleeping tablets to help?'

I immediately reacted with a 'no way'. However, as we discussed further, I agreed that my health was at breaking point and given my private life didn't seem to have a positive 'light at the end of the tunnel' in the near future, perhaps one tablet every now again may help.

That night, after I settled in from a nice warm bath and tucked up in my amazing bed which my mother had gifted me for my 40th birthday, I had a tablet and 9 hours later awoke refreshed, headache free and full of energy.

Aware that this exciting physical and mental feeling was a result of deep sleep, and equally aware not to get lulled into a false sense of security, I embraced the effect. However, I consciously vowed to myself that just one a week was enough to ensure a full rest and would be my absolute limit.

That was 2 years before I left my marriage. As I write this chapter it has been eleven weeks since my marriage ended and insomnia has again become my bed partner. Try as I do with hypnotic meditations, natural supplements and yes ... my 'one a week' tablet ... the heartache, emotional pain, loneliness and heartbreak' are fuelling my sleep deprivation to the point of exhaustion.

It's a part of the process, I get it, however there is no magic that can shake or cure this part of breakdown. As I speak with more women who are opening up to me about their breakdowns, I am finding our common bond in this area. Not one woman has said that from the moment they were able to walk out the door, they have slept deeply and soundly and woken up every morning refreshed!

On the contrary, in all cases it has become worse. So, to some degree I take comfort that I am not alone. The temptation to increase the 'one a week tablet' is real. The lure of making all of the stress and heartbreak disappear for at least a few hours, is strong. I admit, during the last eleven weeks I have had some weeks where, in order to function publicly for work and family I have chosen an extra 'tablet night' from time to time. I'm super careful not to do any more than 2 nights in a week because I know they can 'hook' you in long term. I also know that in the future I will be living in the 'breakthrough stage' of my life and that will be my reward.

As I lay awake last night, after only 3 hours sleep and wishing that my mind would stop having a deep and meaningful conversation with itself, it struck me that I was lonely. I started to sob into my pillow. I knew my husband would not be doing the same. By now I would already have been replaced, doubtless with someone who had already been 'present' during our marriage. My sobs came even more strongly. I even spent some time feeling so sorry for my 'replacement'. I knew full well what they would encounter in time to come. It would be the same as the person before me had experienced too. I secretly wished that I had believed the 'stories' I had been told. Stories that came true.

Then I realized that the only difference between this moment and all those moments prior to eleven weeks ago was that we were living a 'charade' then but now I wasn't. I was just as heartbroken and lonely then. In an instant that realisation stopped my tears. So, did this mean that I had actually taken a step upward and forward and if so, why was there still such deep pain?

As I pondered this, it occurred to me that now I was able to truly process the years and now I could start to take the 'helicopter approach' (flying up and looking down on life playing out below) and analyse what happened. I could start to learn from it all.

I was excited and somewhat curious as to my lack of concern for sleep now at 4.13am! Now was the time for this insomnia to be turned into my 'awake' time … my 'life awake' time. In the stillness of the night, without distractions other than my own thoughts, the opportunity to start to 'rebuild' my life on new foundations that were made of trust, confidence, values, and self-worth was electric!

And so, it begins. The strength of our inner self is powerful and when we have allowed it to be shut down in order to be what others want us to be, or what we think others want us to be, it responds by bringing us to our knees in order to feel it!

As women, especially women over fifty who are filled with so many life experiences, we must remember who we are. We must remember the powerful essence that fuels us and if we have allowed it to be pushed away for any reason, forgive ourselves and seek ways to allow it to resurface. Give ourselves permission to be who we are, in all of our forms. Be unapologetic about living in full authenticity and shine our light on ourselves and others.

So, insomnia, has its purpose. In the silence of the night instead of fighting it and punching the pillows ... start to relax and invite the messages it has for us. As we learn to do this it will slowly drift away as peace and rest is welcomed back into our lives.

Fight or flight?

Relationship breakdowns often have us feeling like we are walking through a different time zone. Before we actually take the step 'out', our minds are filled with the 'What if?' and 'What will happen?' During the step out, equally our minds are in heightened fear and adrenaline wrapped up in confusion and doubt. Then, on the other side, as things start to rearrange themselves in our lives and the newness begins to find its way to our hearts, we experience challenges that we think will be with us forever.

The wonderful news is – they're not permanent! This is where we need to learn to go with the flow. I know ... it's not easy! In fact, because there are usually so many unknowns in the beginning, it's downright damn hard! However, what I do know is that whenever we fight against anything, it actually creates more of it.

Mother Theresa once said, "If you hold an anti-war rally, I shall not attend. But if you hold a Pro-Peace rally invite me.' The reason she said this is she too knew the power of not resisting. When we resist and fight we attract more of what we are resisting and fighting. So, if sleep eludes you, don't fight it. Utilize the awake time for something creative and know that you can sleep more soundly later as a result.

Messages in the silence.

Another thing I recommend when insomnia has taken up residence within you, is to listen. Take the opportunity to listen to what your heart wants to talk to you about. Now, I'm not referring to the negativity and challenges you are currently experiencing in your relationship breakdown because that is your Ego talking. Your heart has so much it wants to share with you. A good way to allow it to speak is to close your eyes and get comfortable. Place your hands on your chest over your heart and your stomach. Take a deep breath in allowing your belly to rise. Then, as you breath out allow it to go down. Do this a few times and in your mind repeat these simple words, 'Breathe in. Breathe out. Breathe in. Breathe out'. Be calm and continue. This is how we are supposed to breathe, filling our belly on the in-breath. Say silently to yourself, 'Breathe in the future. Breathe out the past. Breathe in the future. Breathe out the past'. Continue to do this slowly and gently and after a while just do the breathing and stop speaking to yourself.

Listen to what your heart starts telling you ... let the magic of your life begin!

POINTS TO REMEMBER

* You are going through a form of grief. Your mental and physical health will be taking a heaving load of stress.

* If insomnia or sleep issues start, allow yourself simply to stay awake until you feel really tired.

* Fighting insomnia only increases insomnia.

ACTION STEPS

* Write a list of your favourite podcasts or books and have them ready by your bed. When sleep eludes you, reach for these and enjoy them.

I bring more to others
When I accept and love myself

CHAPTER 8

How to live alone and love it!

I have always been happy with my own company. Having spent a good chunk of my childhood weekends entertaining myself with creative projects, I honestly can't recall feeling unhappy on my own.

As I grew older adult friendship groups came into my life. I always loved spending time with them but I was happy to 'call it quits' long before anyone else was ready to leave. There was always a sense of 'Ok, that's enough time, I have enjoyed the experience and now I want to return to the sanctuary of my home and my personal space.'

After the breakdown of my marriage, I would become upset or lonely at certain times. Times such as when I was driving in my car and it dawned on me that my former partner was at a specific group function that we used to attend together. Or the times on weekends when I would know that he and his new partner were entertaining people in what was once my home, just like we used to.

At these times, I would try and distract the deep pain that was welling in my soul. I would go for a long hard run or reach for a handful of chocolate or a bowl of ice cream to 'stuff it down' further. What I didn't think of was the fact that I actually liked my own company.

I know it was the raw pain of the breakup but it was also the fact that I knew the people my former partner would be with. They were people we had shared happy times with and they would now be hearing a very different story about why we were no longer together. Totally understandable, I would tell myself, because after all my former partner wouldn't want the friends to know the actual truth and in the end it's no one's business except ours.

However, what I have learnt with each breakdown in life is a little 'mental trick' which, the more I practice it the more it works! Having shared this with many clients, I have witnessed incredible results ... simple, easy and effective!

Understanding the power of our subconscious mind,

whenever I find myself in these moments of despair, I tell myself, 'This time next year this moment will be a distant memory and you will not only have moved on. You will be living a life of freedom and possibility that you haven't been able to live for years!' This shifted things and now, when I might otherwise have thought of my former partner in those social situations, I'm ok.

It's a simple statement I know, however, trust me! The more it's repeated the more the subconscious mind embraces it. Honestly, it works. I can personally testify to its power … if only we take the courage to embrace it fully! Please use this little gem anytime you are feeling the same way (especially in the first few months of a breakdown).

When we are in the beginning stages of a breakdown, we forget all of the positive and enlightening things we can do to support our personal growth. So, let me give you this tip based on my experience. Even though it was only temporary I made my home space as beautiful and cosy as I possibly could. I say temporary as initially in a breakup there is a separation of living arrangements. Sometimes through the pain and heartache we can allow the immediate new surroundings to contribute to a build-up of doubt, fear and extra anxiety.

So, looking around where I was living, whilst it wasn't my ideal place I set about making it a representation of what my dream home will have. I made a list of all of the things in every room that I didn't like. Then I went out to different stores and bought replacement items that reflected light, bright, beach life tones.

Simple things like changing the door handles on kitchen cupboards to a beachy wood style and getting whitewash beachy wooden curtain rails with white flowing curtains. I bought cane light shades and bright blue and white cushions of all different shapes for the lounge and beautiful beachy style floor rugs. I didn't buy expensive things because it was temporary and I had to watch my budget. Nonetheless, it all contributed to a beautiful transformation and made the unit feel inviting, warm and nurturing whilst reminding me that my dream home was not that far away. Plus, it was empowering! Empowering because I got to choose the colours, fabrics and styles without having to ask anyone else! I was also able to choose colours that I love that my previous partner had hated and never allowed me to have in the home.

I also bought an essential oil diffuser. I love essential oils and, having trained in the benefits of aromatherapy, I know that each oil can help with emotional healing as well as invigorating mindset! Again, unable to have this for many years due to my previous partner not liking them, it was so exciting that first time I lit the candle and smelt the deep and powerful scent of a healing oil waft throughout my space!

There were so many other things that started to reignite my passion for living just by doing these simple things. Music is at the heart of my life ... always has been. During my relationship I wasn't allowed to have the radio on during the day or encouraged to play music at night. I remember one particular occasion where I thought I was alone in the house and whilst having a shower I put on the radio loud, enjoying the upbeat soul music. All of a sudden, the bathroom door flung open and a raging voice told me to turn it off! Those moments are no longer a part of my life and thankfully, music is once again at the core of my blissful world.

Whilst there are still times that thoughts of what is happening 'somewhere else' brings a heartache, it's now temporary. I understand the value and power of balance between living alone and embracing what life and others have to offer. That balance exhilarates and inspires my soul and I am so pleased to be in this time of my life.

Home is where the heart is!

The clouds of sadness that hang over us during relationship breakdown hide the sunshine that resides above! It is the simple things in life that can make all of the difference. So, when you are in those 'cloudy' times of despair, do the things I have outlined here to make your living space a home and allow that sunshine to come down upon you!

This time next year!

I absolutely LOVE this saying and that is why it is not only the title of this book but also the theme of my 'next step' course and podcast! I use it in almost anything that is a challenge ... not just for relationship breakdown! Four powerful words! I shared them with my gorgeous daughter-in-law as she was going through her labour with her first child, my adorable grandson. Now, understanding and genuinely remembering the physical pain of labour, I do know that words don't help! Hahaha! However, the smile that she gave me and the look on her face let me know that in that moment, some sunshine came into an otherwise tough time! So, feel free to sing it out loud next time you experience the challenges of relationship breakdown and visualize the joy and happiness you will experience ... this time next year!

POINTS TO REMEMBER

* YOU are worthy

* YOU are deserving

* YOU are the most important person in YOUR life

* Pampering yourself is one of the best forms of self-love you can do during this time

ACTION STEPS

*   Write a list of all the pampering experiences you
    would like to explore

My personal pleasure
Comes in many forms
All of which bestow
Great joy

CHAPTER 9

The Sad Vagina ... it's real!

I can't end this simple guidebook without some humour wrapped around the facts! After all, hopefully by now you are feeling more empowered and stronger as you face your challenges.

Another area of our lives that we women over fifty can fear, especially before, during or after a relationship breakthrough is 'Will I ever find love again?' or 'Will there ever be someone out there for me?' As I write this chapter, I can say with absolute commitment another relationship is currently THE furthest thing from my mind. However, I am not dead yet and I am buoyed by the fact that my heroines such as Jane Fonda and Kathy Lette continue to inspire women on this front too!

You know how when things aren't going right in your life and your body reacts? I've already talked about the emotional eating habit that can trigger a whole wave of other regrets other than the one you're emotionally eating for in the first place. Louise Hay's #1 best-selling book *You Can Heal Your Life!* demonstrates this point. As you turn each page, she outlines the different emotions and challenges we encounter and what part of the body is affected and even has a full A, B, C dictionary-style reference at the back for quick answers to what really ails us! It's brilliant and my copy is never too far away!

Well … let me tell you a story about the 'Sad Vagina'. Whenever I have been in a relationship and I have had the strong instinct that something was wrong (trust me, my next book is going to be titled *How to Trust Your Instincts and Get the Hell Out of There Now!)* my body has started to react.

'Gut instincts' which cause constipation, the runs, insomnia, mind chatter of the 'what ifs' are all examples of our body sending a message to our minds. In tough times my body has always expressed an interesting reaction which I have learnt is its way of telling a woman, 'Just go! It's done! You are not loved here!'. Depending on my strength and ability to take its advice – which then determines how long I drag the inevitable out – here is what my body does.

I have always loved making love. I love the physical contact, the feeling of loving and being loved. The sense of being wanted by another and being able to express that back. I have enjoyed everything that our physical bodies are designed to give and receive. What I have noticed is that when the relationship is going in the wrong direction, so does my desire. Nothing unusual you might say however many women don't realise this. Many women fear what lies 'beyond the relationship' and stay in their 'comfort zone' but their desire evaporates and then they seek professional advice assuming there is something else wrong with them.

How do I know this? It has happened to me and since my most recent breakup I have learnt it happens to women everywhere!

For me, it started when I discovered the issues occurring in the relationship. It was like my subconscious mind said, 'Right then, we're not going to enjoy anything now so we will just switch of your happiness button for a while'. Because there was a huge slice of 'denial and hope' I ignored this and reluctantly continued in the physical side of the relationship.

The challenge was that my subconscious was clearly confused as it had already sent a directive! So, my body starts to experience intimacy pain. That then sends a message that because there is pain something is wrong. So, I sought medical advice. The doctor suggested I see a specialist. The specialist said, 'You are menopausal so start using these medications and that will fix it'. It didn't and the pain increased so now began the excuses and delay tactics in intimate encounters. Now, at this stage you are probably thinking, 'Why didn't you just leave given you knew the betrayal was happening and the relationship was doomed instead of enduring the pain?' That's just it, the pain of leaving was overtaking the physical pain associated with staying.

Things went from bad to worse. It got to the point where it was so horrid, that side of life simply stopped. I told myself I was at that age where the drive goes and that I didn't really care anyway. I also told myself that I wasn't that attractive so more than happy not to beat myself up anymore.

Well, here is the twist! Whenever I have had a relationship breakdown and some healing time has passed ... I feel 'great' again!

I was sharing this with my girlfriend recently and she said, 'You just had a 'Sad Vagina.' After seeing my totally confused face she laughed and said, 'It's real! Don't look confused! Research has shown that when a woman's heart is broken, particularly where betrayal has occurred, their vaginas are affected. They just "switch off", causing massive pain if you try to "switch it back on"!'

I laughed so hard I started to cry!!! She was right! Mine was so sad throughout the horrible final months! I couldn't wait to Google it and sure enough! There are so many research papers and studies all proving that it is real!

So, one of the goals for we women over fifty who have

summoned the courage to breakout of the breakdown is to step back into our true, amazing powerful selves and say goodbye to the 'Sad Vagina' and hello to life again!

The happy vagina!

Now that I have shared my 'personals' with you and you have stopped laughing at this revelation, it's time to get 'Happy' again! Hopefully this enlightening chapter fills you with excitement – not too much yet – get your relationship breakdown sorted – and then get ready for life again!. There is much to look forward to in your future! However, if your sex life isn't something that you are too concerned with, that's fine. Just know that if something changes, THAT'S ok too!

Laughter and smiling – a winning combination!

In case you are at that point in your relationship breakdown where sadness is overbearing and you can't find joy in anything, I totally understand.

Relationship breakdown is like the death of a loved one. The stress and pain within are exactly the same. We don't feel like laughing, smiling or having fun when someone we have loved so deeply passes.

I know that the months leading up to my mother's death and indeed that day itself, the last thing I felt like doing was having a belly laugh. I did the absolute opposite. After I waited by her side for the undertakers to take her away, I went down to the beach at the end of our street. It was a very hot day. We were in the middle of a massive heat wave and it was about 40C. I removed my shoes and deliberately walked across the hot, burning sand so I could feel the pain. I entered the still, glass-like water and I slowly walked out into the sea. The water came up to my waist and then it was chest deep. In that moment, in that very painful and numb moment, I could have easily kept walking and never looked back, so deep was the heartache and pain. However, in that final moment as the water rose to below my chin, I heard my mother's voice say, 'This time next year ... '

Try and find things in your day that make you smile. Maybe it is a favourite song on the radio, or a comedy show you enjoy on TV. Perhaps it is simply the sound of a child laughing as they walk past you. Turn on your 'heart radar' and seek it out then put it all in your 'soul bank' to withdraw in the moments of pain.

POINTS TO REMEMBER

* Life may not be all 'roses and buttercups' right now however, trust me, the 'new you' has so much to look forward too.

* If you are feeling like you're not happy with yourself right now, that is ok, however again … trust me … the 'new you' has SO much to look forward

* Laughter is one of THE best forms of therapy!

ACTION STEPS

* Start watching comedies and movies that are
  fun!

* Re read this chapter and have a good old laugh!

When we have the clarity of
Who we are
And the courage to
See ourselves in all our glory
We are complete and therefore
We are perfect

CHAPTER 10

Courage, clarity, complete!

Whilst this is the final chapter in my 'This Time Next Year' guidebook gift to you, it is not the end of what you are currently going through. No matter where you are in your relationship breakdown or the crossroads of your life, there will still be times of challenge and uncertainty. There will no doubt be moments of anger, regret, fear and depression.

However this much I do know ... you are stronger, more resourceful, more empowered in this moment than you have ever been before! How do I know this? Because I have been where you are right now and if I had been stronger, more resourceful and more empowered before this moment … I wouldn't have been in this relationship breakdown.

What I have come to realise is that I am a courageous, empowered, caring, resilient and resourceful woman, however, whilst I thought I had embodied those qualities I hadn't cleared the negative emotions and beliefs on a subconscious level that had built up over the years of my relationship and as a result they created the blocks in my life that stopped me from growing and learning.

We are always learning and growing. The key is to be aware of when we are growing and embrace these times within us so that we can call on the strength we gain when we need them.

I have given you some steps and tips that will help you, if you choose. I have read books, gone to seminars, attended workshops, listened to podcasts and one thing I know for sure – I have always had the choice as to whether to take what was being taught and act on it or not.

No one can magically take away the pain of a relationship breakdown or give you the exact steps to move you forward when you are at a crossroads in your life. We are not victims here when we understand that we have the ability to turn the breakdown in our life into our own amazing breakthrough. What is important, is for us to find our way to what we want our breakthrough to be and look like.

By following the ideas and steps within this book, you can

begin to create an exciting path to follow. It's your personal 'This Time Next Year' guidebook and you can tailor it to fit exactly with where you are now.

The **3 Main Steps** that I like to remind myself of throughout a breakdown are:

* I am courage and I have all the courage of a lioness within me!

* I am clarity and I can see everything for what it is and how I can best use it for creative solutions!

* I am complete. I am whole and perfect just the way I am! I love myself deeply!

I am honoured that you chose to have me join you at this important time in your life. I trust that the words I have shared have helped where they needed to and that you are feeling stronger and wiser as a result.

This is just the beginning. This book is the first of many that are combined with the companion course – 'This Time Next Year ... Your Roadmap to Your New Life' and Podcast Series – 'This Time Next Year – The Podcast'.

Our time together can continue and I invite you to let me know how you are going because I want to know!

You can contact me through my personal website www. jayniemorris.com or social media and of course tag yourself with where you are at using the hashtags #ThisTimeNextYear and #TransformingNOWTogetherWithJaynieMorris

My free 4-week online course *'This Time Next Year'* is available from my website www.jayniemorris.com

It will guide you through what to do over 28 days for every aspect of your life that you need in this moment. It features experts interviewed by me on the areas we train on each week. The workbook is free to download and is an exciting addition to this book. The course has been designed to help you at wherever your life breakdown is. Relationship, career, health, personal or – the big one we women over 50 have – 'Where am I going in life?'

Finally, from my heart to yours ... I do know how you are feeling right now.

I have been there. I know the fear and pain and torture of the lonely nights. I understand the confusion and the anger that occurs from 'the other side' too. What I do know is, if you are willing to embrace the pain and change in order to move from the crossroads to clarity and from feeling empty to empowered then, just like me, you WILL move from your Breakdown to the most incredible Breakthrough in your life ... This Time Next Year!

I send you love and heart hugs!

POINTS TO REMEMBER

* YOU are stronger, more resourceful, more empowered in this moment than you have ever been before!

* You have in your hands a 'guidebook' written by someone who has been in your situation ... take courage and clarity from each page.

* Every day will be different. How you deal with it will determine how it will end.

ACTION STEPS

* Keep in touch with me. Subscribe on my website www.jayniemorris.com

* Explore the companion online course on my website that will give you more information and support

* Reread this book often, you will 'see' things that you missed in the first reading that may help you

* Consider attending one of my companion workshops and/or retreats when you are ready

I don't understand, I'm confused.
What is it that you want from me?
I don't know how to 'be'.
We are equal, yes?
Then why do I feel you don't like me?

Boys and men — part of the solution

I remember as a child, enjoying and loving interactions with boys in conversation. As I grew up, I often reflect on how I found it easier to talk to guys than women. I sometimes wonder if that was due to an underlying lack of self-esteem that I held within, never showing to the 'outside' world. When it came to talking with women, I always felt I wasn't pretty enough, smart enough, or as 'good' as they appeared to be. However, when it came to men, I never seemed to have that issue.

Certainly, as my business career developed, I revelled in the conversations of strategy, development, ideas and inspiration. As I write this sentence, I again find myself somewhat in that 'zone'! Clearly it comes naturally and ignites a passion so perhaps it's because I felt at ease with like-minded individuals? I am not sure.

However, what I am sure of is that over time, due to the definite inequality and 'lesser than us' culture that women have had to endure, there has developed another 'casualty' that has been overlooked.

As our voices rise in protest and demand positive change and equality, all 100% rightfully so, my passion for these increases. I strongly believe that once we have achieved the 'balance' that we all need, the benefits to both women and men are going to be enormous.

This is what I would like to shine a light on here and continue to incorporate in all that I do moving forward.

You see, as a mother of two wonderful adult sons, grandmother to a magical grandson, now a partner of an incredible new man in my life and friend of countless men around the world, I see the role of my work to also consider their welfare, mental health and personal growth very seriously.

If we exclude men from the conversation, then we are discounting the millions of men around the world who are amazing, kind, generous, respectful and loving of the women in their lives. We run the risk of always having blocks on our roads to equality, purely through removing these men from the conversations.

Yes, there are men who are narcissistic, disrespectful, abusive, manipulative, deceitful and selfish. I know this all too well having lived with one. We all know this!

However, what of the men who are empathic, encouraging, flexible, honest and generous? What can we women do to ensure that our sons, grandsons and future generations of men feel safe enough to share their feelings in a respectful and kind way?

What can we women do to include them, teach them and create a future where they understand and love us as we deserve. One where we can do the same in return.

That is ultimately what we are seeking, yes?

Equality on all levels, wrapped up in mutual respect, kindness, consideration, inclusion, support and all the many elements that make for positive lives.

My lived experience was one of feeling I needed to 'justify' to others my decision to leave my husband and then the consequent pain of being 'unheard' and not believed by many.

Once I had worked through the emotional brutality of this, I started to have conversations with men in my inner circle. I then extended it to my male friends and colleagues in business and friendships around the world. I also included my beautiful male gay friends, to help me understand the dark side I had encountered with another.

With every conversation, I asked questions such as 'How do you feel about women?'; 'What are your thoughts on equal rights?'; 'Do you think women should be paid the same as men and why?'; 'In a relationship with women, what concerns you the most about communication?'; 'Have you ever encountered an abusive relationship?'; 'What does domestic abuse mean to you?' and so on.

With every conversation, a pattern started to unfold. There were some who answered predictably because they were and have always been very self-secure and confident. Their concerns about abuse, betrayal, lies, coercive control and manipulation of others were passionate.

Equally, their frustration at being 'sandwiched' was also very evident. The Sandwich Generation of men have lived through a period of rapid change full of double standards and mixed messages. They have waded through layers of cultural conditioning and expectations that were rapidly being changed and broken down.

Previous generations had what some would call a 'clear stereotype' for men and women to follow.

Now, before you think 'That is the problem! That is why we women are suffering today' please pause. I agree with you. However, let's not forget that this 'stereotype' conditioning plays an enormous role in the breakdown of men's ability to cope and understand how to communicate on an equal basis. How to interact in a safe and equal level. You can fill in the gaps of this long list!

In the podcasts and panel discussions I have been involved in that focus on the challenges, issues and sometimes horrific abuse experienced by women of all ages, a 'common thread' of behaviours is exhibited by the perpetrators. And the recognition of those behaviours by the members of the audience who I see nodding confirms this. I also receive messages from listeners who say 'That happened to me. That was exactly what was done to me.'

The more I read and saw these responses, I couldn't help but ask the question, 'Have all the perpetrators of domestic abuse around the world gone to the same school? Are they all 'trained' by someone to act in the same way?' Stay with me here before you get triggered as that isn't my intention. Think about it. Whenever you have read an article or heard a lived experience account, haven't you also thought this?

So, this is why I want to include boys and men in our conversation and for men to be a part of the solution for us all. After all, more often than not they are a part of the problem. Let's find a way to deal with this so that current and future generations have a clarity, an understanding, a pathway forward for respectful, loving and healthy relationships.

I want to contribute to the solution to the huge inequality that exists between men and women in our current generations. I want to find the way forward so that this important step in the healing and improvement of what is clearly a pandemic of pain, suffering and desperate times, can be done now ... in this time ... for us and with us all.

How do we do that? It's not an easy question nor answer. However, education is a great place to start. In my research I am finding incredible resources and organisations that are supporting men of all ages especially in the space of mental health.

In Australia, one of my favourites is The Man Cave. These words on their website jolted me upright.

'We exist because suicide is the leading cause of death for men aged 15-44. It's not car crashes, drug overdoses or coward punches. The biggest killer of young men is themselves. Not only that, more than one woman dies every week at the hands of a man and most of the time this is a man they're close with, someone they trust.' The Man Cave's focus on is making a difference and I encourage everyone to check them out. Full details in the Resource section.

My good friend, Jamie Milne of JMT Training, has been a guest on my podcasts and is passionate about change especially for young boys and men in the mental health space. His personal story is not only inspiring it is a great 'map to follow' in the times of darkness and despair. Again, his details are in the Resources section and I encourage you to visit the Podcast section of www.jayniemorris.com to check out our chats together!

These two resources are just the tip of the iceberg so I have listed more resources and links at the end of this book that may be of interest. I invite you to check them out. Meantime, let's make sure that as we work on ourselves, we don't forget that there are many good men, among the hordes of great women, who want to see us succeed and are willing to support us to do so. The more we help each other, the brighter our future.

There are many more available, too many to include, however what I encourage you to do is explore, ask, and seek out help no matter what is going on in your life. When you find yourself in the deep depths of despair you may feel, as I did, that there was nowhere to go and no help available. It is easy for our mind to play that trick and keep us locked up in the breakdown phase of our lives. That is when you have a choice ... you either continue to allow the chains that have been placed around you to tighten and keep you from moving forward or you can find that empowered strength that is always inside you and pull it out to bring you to the breakthrough that you so deserve.

POINTS TO REMEMBER

* Not all men are alike

* Read that again

* Not all men are alike

* Just like we women, men are also a product of their environments, cultures and social conditioning.

* As women, we do play a vital role in educating and supporting the younger generations of men

* It's easy to say 'that's not our job' however the reality is that we women know deep down that if we are to have the cycles 'broken' and positive futures for our communities in the future, then we are the ones to take on that role.

ACTION STEPS

* Write a list of all the males throughout your
  life that you have had a good relationship/
  connection with

* Next to each name, write 2 things that make you
  smile when you think of them.

* If you were asked to contribute to changing
  negative male behaviour, what would you want
  changed … and how do you think that would
  benefit men in their lives.

MY RESOURCES

Our time together continues! You are going to always want to be a part of this evolving, international community now ... trust me ... the best is YET to come!

I am so honoured that you have read this book to this point. You are going through so many changes, I totally understand that and remember this point in my own life all too well.

There will be days of deep despair, when you feel like there is no hope and you are gripped with emotional pain. There will be days of absolute joy and gratitude as some of the areas that I have highlighted in this guidebook – show themselves to you and you receive the benefits.

The 'rollercoaster' will be ongoing for a while however hopefully this guidebook and our coming together will contribute to great outcomes and a faster approach to you being in the healthy, happy and peaceful state that you deserve.

My website space – www.jayniemorris.com – is a must to SUBSCRIBE so that we can stay connected PLUS follow throughout all my social media!

My online 'companion' 4-week course to this book is so important to explore as I have included other independent experts and support information that will complement what you have here.

My workshops, both in person and online, are also designed to add strength and education for you to become the best version of you and give you pathways to your new life.

My retreats are magical! They are each different and are either 2 or 7 days. Every day is filled with nurturing, healthy activities that will have you 'floating home' in a bubble of total self-love and pampering.

All of these have been designed to support you as you move towards the exciting new chapter in your life. I have designed them all to be what I as a survivor and person who has been where you are, would want to have moving forward.

I am excited that you may well explore and attend all or some of these too, for that means you are committed to being happy, healthy and joyful more than ever before! That is my personal wish for you too xxx

RESOURCES TO ASSIST IN TIMES OF CRISIS

Centrelink. Don't be too proud or allow guilt or shame to prevent you from this vital step. And don't let the delays often encountered with this service put you off from finding out what is available to you and what services they can provide in your time of need – www.servicesaustralia.gov.au. If you are reading this outside of Australia, find out what is the equivalent to Centrelink in your country.

UnitingCare is an Australian organization that provides incredible support on many levels including (at the time of writing this book) the delivery of the EVP program which supports women who flee domestic violence. www.uca.org.au

The Leichhardt Women's Community Health Centre was one of the pivotal organisations that saved my mental distress when I discovered the betrayal in my relationship. At the time of writing, it is the only organization in Australia that supports women who discover that their male partners are gay and that they (the women) have been used as 'beards'. The discovery of this in a relationship has more than just mental and emotional consequences. It potentially carries physical issues that require immediate attention. They provide counselling, information and support groups for women in this situation and were invaluable to me.

www.respect.gov.au is a good service provided by the Australian government and again, in other countries please seek out the equivalent.

www.lifeline.org.au have wonderful counsellors and can help direct you to the services where you live that you may need. Phone 13 11 14 for support.

Catherine House is a South Australia organization that offers support and trauma informed care and accommodation for women experiencing homelessness www.catherinehouse. org.au.

Mission Australia also provides support around homelessness. There are many organisations now supporting people in this area so a quick google search in your local area can assist www.missionaustralia.com.au.

It's important to remember that I don't have all of the answers and it is up to you to seek out in your local area what is available however there is always help ... sometimes we just don't realise it.

Did I mention I love reading and podcasts! Apart from my own books and podcasts that is hahaha! (Remember to subscribe at www.jayniemorris.com so you never miss any episodes!)

The following are some of my personal favourites. I recommend these for you to consider as well ... you can never have too much support or too many options right!

BOOKS & PODCASTS

'HRT – Husband Replacement Therapy' by the amazing Kathy Lette (you may recognize a cameo appearance as a 'character' in this book too)

'You Are the Guru' by Gabby Bernstein

'Change your Thoughts – Change Your Life' by Dr Wayne Dyer

'Abundance Now!' by Lisa Nichols

'Finding My Balloon' by Kathleen Shapona

'Finally Find the Love of Your Life' by Jenny Schmal

'90 Seconds to a Life You Love' by Dr Joan Rosenberg

'Braving The Wilderness' by Brene Brown

'Life & Love – creating the dream' by Lisa Messenger

Mel Robbins Podcast

Jay Shetty Podcast

Dr Joe Dispenza Podcast

RESOURCES RELEVANT TO MEN'S LIVED EXPERIENCE

Michael Ray is an Australian guy making great inroads with gender equity. He is a solo dad, author, speaker and advocate for equality and change. I include him on this list as it's incredibly important to be equally supportive on every level to the boys and men in our lives as it is girls and women ... for all of the reasons I have listed in my bonus chapter. www.michaelray.com.au

The Man Cave is another favourite of mine for boys. I have already stated the reasons in the bonus chapter however it is worth repeating, 'They exist because suicide is the leading cause of death for men aged 15-44. It's not car crashes, drug overdoses or coward punches. The biggest killer of young men is themselves. Not only that, more than 1 woman dies every week at the hands of a man and most of the time this is a man they're close with ... someone they trust.' The Man Cave programmes and support are focused on changing this www.themancave.life

These are resources that I discovered along my journey. I share them with you in the hope that these may help you along the way too. They're focused on Australia so if you are reading this in another country, please seek the equivalent organisations. I would love to know about them so please send their details to info@jayniemorris.com with 'This Time Next Year – International Support' in the SUBJECT line.

GratitudePlus

This is where the 'acknowledgements' go when an Author puts pen to paper and creates a book.

For me, 'acknowledgements' is not quite how I feel about the following people ... it is so much more than that. The list is huge and I am hoping for this particular book I have remembered all of the valued people I want to spread 'GratitudePlus' on.

Firstly, and most importantly, my two sons Benjamin and Nathan. These two incredible humans have taught me life lessons that usually others provide when you are 'growing up'. They came into my life when I was very young and whilst with any family, we have had our fair share of ups and downs, without them I wouldn't be here today.

To my daughter-in-law, Summer, for loving my son and being a beautiful light in life. She is the daughter I never had and always wished for. To my divine grandson Leon ... you are simply magical and THE love of my life. The gift of love you radiate constantly is so very powerful.

To my editors and contributors especially the incredibly talented Michaela Andreyev. Thank you for your support, guidance, elegant expertise and talent. Thank you for the steadying hands, no 'holding back' and honest partnership that will be enduring and continuing for many years to come.

To my incredible sisterhood who, with their wisdom, advice, support and unconditional love, ensured that I never gave up ... always remembered the light within me ... and fuelled my return to life – Traci, Julie, Kathleen, Anna, Elle, Carol, Suzanne, Cheryl, Pat, Cassandra, Kate, Deb, Cherrie, Antoinette, Maria, Janine and Mel Dee xxxxx

To my greater group of friends who have shared the years, the tears, the laughs and the fun ... may we all get to do more in the coming years!

To the incredible Therese Robson who through her support, expertise and genuine commitment to helping women in domestic abuse situations ... you are much loved.

To my wonderful Team at both SheroesUnlimited and TransformingNOWTogether with Jaynie Morris. A very special 'GratitudePlus' to Jason and Aby who masterfully help everything I do look great and present perfectly so that our work together for others always holds value. Roslyn Foo – timing is everything and you are the magical timing for me xx

To my clients who place their lives in my hands every session and trust me to take them on a journey of empowered improvement wrapped up in real strategies.

To all my ExPartners, including my favourite and very much missed father of my children, Rick. Every moment spent with each one of you has been a gift; sometimes clearly seen and at other times it took me a while! However, without exception, you shaped the woman I am today and for that I am truly grateful.

To Peter, who through his 'flipping' relationship pathways on its head … showed me how real caring, thoughtfulness, trust, support, communication and unconditional love is supposed to be. Writing our next life chapter together is already adventure filled.

Finally, to my Mum and Dad. Thank you for deciding to have that 'last ditch' moment of passion that resulted in me!

And thank you to me … for having the courage and strength to start to 'relisten' to my intuition which resulted in the foundation of this book … understanding that EVERY Breakdown is a stepping stone up to an incredible Breakthrough! And that focusing on 'This Time Next Year' is the true pathway to freedom and life fulfillment!

ABOUT THE AUTHOR

As a survivor of domestic abuse, Jaynie brings to every conversation and every opportunity the wisdom that is only created as a result of 'lived experience.' Having endured and experienced it all, she is committed to contributing to change. Change and education of our future generations in understanding how the behaviour of domestic abuse, in particular narcissistic behaviour, is not tolerated and provide pathways and tools to ensure generational domestic abuse stops.

Jaynie is a woman who never gives up. Despite the challenges that we all face in life, many of which have brought her personally to her knees, she has 'eternal optimism' running through her veins and that is what fuels her purpose in life.

She is a mother, grandmother and friend to many around the world. She is an author (clearly – you've just read her book!), survivor, speaker, Master Trainer, life coach, dabbles as a casual yoga Instructor and lover of all things wellbeing!

She's experienced incredible heights in business internationally and hit rock bottom in equal measure. She's exuded inspiration and motivation on stage to audiences from 50 – 5000+, and had times of sobbing into the early hours of the morning believing that there was no more life to give.

In 2012 Jaynie was given the devastating prognosis of potentially only 2 months to live after an ongoing pain in her stomach was diagnosed as 87% of her liver being dead. She dug into her deep well of courage and resources which culminated in a full recovery and living an active jam-packed life. This experience was well documented in her book 'Against Their Odds' which gained national and international media coverage and had her supporting others worldwide on their health journeys.

Founder & Owner of SheroesUnlimited – a Global Community for women over fifty and 'Jaynie Morris – TransformingNOWTogether' – Jaynie is an unapologetic advocate for the empowerment of women over fifty. More importantly Jaynie has become a passionate Advocate and Activist for Unity and is fiercely focused on achieving this worldwide! Constantly speaking, training and working with women and men who seek positive change and authentic results in their lives, Jaynie helps create pathways and strategies for overall life success.

Having spent a considerable portion of life living and working around the world, Jaynie now lives in Australia with her family and very close-knit sisterhood!

Jaynie can be contacted through Jaynie Morris – TransformingNOWTogether www.jayniemorris.com or any of her social media

Twitter – @morrisjaynie

Facebook – www.facebook.com/
JaynieMorrisTransformingNOWTogether

Instagram – @jayniemorris

Email connection – info@jayniemorris.com

To invite Jaynie to speak at your event please email details to
info@jayniemorris.com or visit www.jayniemorris.com and go
to the 'Invite Jaynie To Speak'

WOULD YOU LIKE TO DO MORE?

1:1 COACHING – I love to help women and men break down the barriers in their lives and become empowered, happy and fulfilled! Each year I open up a small number of Client Opportunities for online consults, so if you would like to clear negative emotions and beliefs and rediscover YOU, then simply checkout the link on my website at www.jayniemorris. com or email info@jayniemorris.com

ONLINE COACHING & COURSES – Working with an international team of experts in various fields, we have created several online courses that you can do at your own pace, in your own time and on your own terms! Visit www. jayniemorris.com and explore the options available now!

WORKSHOPS – I have developed both in person and online workshops that work in conjunction with this book. They are designed to take you to the next level. Information available at my website www.jayniemorris.com or email info@ jayniemorris.com for our next ones available.

RETREATS – Ready to do some self-nurturing? Time for you to be pampered? I have designed 2 and 7 day retreats that do that and SO much more! Every day is filled with a focus of relaxation, pampering and rejuvenation. Visit my website www.jayniemorris.com or email info@jayniemorris.com requesting information on our upcoming retreats.

INVITE ME TO SPEAK – With over 35-years-experience globally in the Motivational & Inspirational Industry, sharing my story – sharing ideas, well researched strategies and more – being part of positive and sustainable transformation – empowering others through powerful education – these are all the things I love to do in life. Check out the 'Invite Jaynie To Speak' at www.jayniemorris.com for more information on how we can work together today. Or send me an email to info@ jayniemorris.com

I am personally represented by Australian Speakers Bureau – all details www.australianspeakersbureau.com